A CONTRARY HISTORY OF THE WEST
AND OTHER ESSAYS

Roger Sworder

A CONTRARY HISTORY
OF THE WEST

And Other Essays

SOPHIA PERENNIS

SAN RAFAEL, CA

First published in the USA
by Sophia Perennis
© Roger Sworder 2011

Series editor: James R. Wetmore

For information, address:
Sophia Perennis, P.O. Box 151011
San Rafael, CA 94915
sophiaperennis.com

Library of Congress Cataloging-in-Publication Data

Sworder, Roger.
A contrary history of the West: and other essays / Roger Sworder.

p. cm.

Includes bibliographical references.
ISBN 978-1-59731-130-4 (pbk: alk. paper)
1. Philosophy. I. Title
B 29.S88   2011
190—dc22   2001018283

CONTENTS

ACKNOWLEDGEMENTS

Thanks to the following people for editing and publishing earlier versions of essays in this book. Eugenia Mitrakas and David Roylance for *The Origin of One Greek Games* and *The Metaphysics of Professional Life*; John Penwill for *The Portland Vase, Plato's Number of Justice,* and *Plato's Song of the Sirens*; Tim Scott for *Three Short Essays in Astrophysiology*; and the editors of "Quadrant" for *Gravity as Harmony* and *A Manifesto for the Humanities*. Without the care of Dorothy Avery this book would not exist.

INTRODUCTION

What is the world made of? According to Plato, the ideas by which we interpret the physical world are much more real than the physical world. He thought that ideas such as unity, plurality and equality were eternal beings and that they were causes of the things in the physical world. From the modern standpoint, Plato put this the wrong way round. From our standpoint, our experiences of things through our senses are the origin of our ideas of those things. We abstract our ideas of things from the things we experience in the world through our senses. Ideas come after things.

Plato had an argument against abstraction. In a crowd of people, each person is one person among other people. But each person also has many parts, such as legs and arms. Again, my ring finger is smaller than my middle finger but bigger than my little finger. Finger and person 'roll around' between big and small, one and many, and appear in opposite ways at different times from different points of view. These properties are not fixed, but contextual. How then could anyone ever abstract the idea of big or small, one or many, from these ambiguous things? These ideas cannot be abstracted from things because a thing may always be seen as one or many, big or small.

Surprisingly, the philosophical name for Plato's view of ideas is Realism. Realism is the theory that some ideas are real beings beyond time and space but informing what is in time and space. There are many other ways in which the ancients took what we regard as abstract notions for real things and causes. The dispositions of the solar system were the musical intervals of the diatonic octave. Dusk was a sexual union, dawn a birth. The parts of the human body realized the Zodiacal constellations.

Contemplation of these analogies had spiritual force since the patterns were themselves gods and goddesses. So Aphrodite embodied the identity between the union of light and night at sunset when

1

her star appeared, and the sexual union of male and female. Venus is goddess of dusk and goddess of love. Gods and goddesses were patterns of metaphor coordinating widely divergent dimensions in mutually revealing ways. Contemplation of the patterns induced awe and generated many forms of worship.

Many of the essays in this book are studies of this metaphoric realism. In some of them both parts of the analogy or metaphor are physical, as with sunset and sexual union. Here all the elements of the pattern are easily understood. Such patterns are forgotten ways of relating physical things to each other, ways very different from the quantifications of our present science. But these ancient patterns are just as mathematically exact. A metaphor survives on its exactitude:

> Their scorn had all the effect on him of a light frost on a polar bear.

The analogies between planets and musical tones, Venus and love, Zodiac and human body are precise. They are all exact measurings of one dimension against another, but measurings much more flexible and imaginative than numerical counting.

Not all metaphors are real in the philosophical sense. They are not all gods and goddesses at the heart of things. The metaphor of the polar bear is not real in this sense. Real or not, metaphors have no exclusive claim on the things they relate. Every god and goddess is a pattern connecting many things, but there is always the rest of the pantheon and what they connect. Polarities such as male and female, light and dark, may even be reversed in some instances in different patterns, so that two real metaphors may be logically incompatible. These essays do not offer a unified theory of everything. They are more unified than most in just one respect. They reunite the metaphors of poetry with the rhythms of statuary and the intervals of the musical scale, with the movements of the stars and the ratios of Euclidean geometry. In these essays, art and science are not divided.

1

THE ORIGIN
OF ONE GREEK GAMES

There are few things as Greek as the Olympic Games are Greek. That athletic contests come down to us from the ancient Greeks in the first instance, no one denies. As to when and why the practice originated, no one claims to know. These questions seem impossible to answer. The traditional date for the founding of the Olympic Games is 776 BC but there is general agreement that there were some such games at Olympia long before this. At the very beginning of our era, Homer's *Odyssey* already describes the practice of games as very widespread, when the insulting Euryalus says to Odysseus in Phaeacia:

> Well I, at least, stranger, do not suppose you to be a man trained in athletic contests such as abound among mankind.[1]

Phaeacia is, geographically, the last outpost of humanity in the Ocean but the Phaeacians, too, have their games with many of the Olympic events. So we may say that from the ancient Greek point of view the practice of the games was immemorially old, old by the time of Homer, old by the time of Odysseus.

We cannot say when the games originated and we cannot say why. They were certainly one form of funerary celebrations, for example the games in *Iliad XXIII* at the funeral of Patroclus and those in *Aeneid V* at the funeral of Anchises. Games were held in honour of heroes, Melicertes in the Isthmus, Pelops at Olympia, but whether they were in all cases funerary memorials is impossible to

1. Homer, *Odyssey*, VIII, 159–160.

3

tell. And of course, the games were consecrated to Gods, Zeus at Olympia, Poseidon in the Isthmus, Apollo at Delphi. But why the Greeks should have chosen to worship their Gods and honour their heroes in this way is quite obscure. It certainly looks as though these first questions we ask about the origins of the Games, when and why, are going to fail of an answer.

But there is one early account of an early games which tells us exactly how those games originated. The account is given by Herodotus, writing about 450 BC. He is describing the origin of certain Etruscan games, ordained by the Delphic oracle about 540 BC and held regularly from that time to Herodotus' own. To understand Herodotus' story we need to go back a little before 540 BC when these Etruscan games were founded. In 559 BC Cyrus came to the throne of the Medes and Persians, and he marched west. The Greek cities on the seaboard of Asia Minor were among his targets and Delphi counselled the Greeks in Asia Minor to withdraw and to recolonize in the west, in Italy and southern France, rather than submit to Cyrus. The Greek islanders on Teos and the citizens of Phocaea were alone among the Eastern Greeks to adopt this policy. Somewhat less than half the citizens of Phocaea migrated to Corsica and re-established themselves there in a colony called Alalia which they had founded about 565 BC. But this enlarged Corsican colony of Greeks was attacked by neighboring Carthaginians and Etruscans who sailed against the colony with sixty ships each. The Greeks with sixty ships met them in the Sea of Sardinia and forced their retreat. This was the greatest Mediterranean sea battle of the sixth century BC and a Greek victory although they were outnumbered two to one.

Here is Herodotus:

For five years [the new immigrants] lived at Alalia with the former settlers and built temples in the town; but during that period they caused so much annoyance to their neighbors by plunder and pillage, that the Etruscans and Carthaginians agreed to attack them with a fleet of sixty ships apiece. The Phocaeans manned their own vessels, also sixty in number, and sailed to meet them in the Sardinian sea, as it is called. In the engagement which followed the Phocaeans won; but it was a Cadmeian sort of victory with more loss than gain, for forty of their vessels were destroyed and the remaining twenty had their rams so badly bent as to render them unfit for service. The survivors returned to Alalia, took aboard their women and children and such of their property as there was room for, and sailed from Corsica to Rhegium. The Carthaginians and Etruscans drew lots for the possession of the prisoners from the ships which were sunk. Of the Etruscans, the people of Agylla got by far the largest number, and they took them all ashore and stoned them to death. The result of this outrage was that when any living thing—sheep, ox, or man—subsequently passed the place where the Phocaeans had lain, its body became twisted and crippled by a paralytic stroke. Wishing to expiate the crime of the murder, the men of Agylla sent to Delphi, and were told by the Priestess to begin the custom, which they still observe today, of honouring the dead men with a grand funeral ceremony and the holding of athletic and equestrian contests.[2]

At first sight Herodotus' narrative is straightforward, each event or action following from the last. In this account of the inauguration of the games we seem to understand what is happening and we note that these games were not merely approved but enjoined by the Delphic oracle, the greatest single authority of the ancient Greek world. But we note that 'the athletic and equestrian contests' sound much more like the Olympic games than the Delphic games. The Delphic games included musical as well as athletic contests. The Olympic games, like these Etruscan games, had no musical contests. We must now ask why Apollo at Delphi authorized these games, which is a much sharper, clearer and more answerable question than the question of why there were games at all.

Even so we run into difficulties, of two different kinds: Herodotus' narrative turns on the supernatural destruction wrought at the scene of the massacre; and it concerns the international relations between Greeks and Etruscans. In the case of the supernatural we

---

2. Herodotus, *The Histories*, I, 165–166.

can find a parallel from the same place and period which shows how a murdered man of some distinction made the crime against him known. About 500 BC the poet Ibycus of Rhegium, on his way to a festival, was murdered by highwaymen. The highwaymen then attended the festival themselves. Sitting together in the amphitheater they were singled out and subjected to continuous attack by two cranes. After this terrifying experience they quickly admitted their crime. Something comparable to this is happening in the account of Agylla in Etruria in Herodotus' story, but there is a cultural war being waged here too. Etruscans tended to sacrifice prisoners of war to their gods, though there is no mention of sacrifice in the murder of the sailors. But killing prisoners is generally against Greek practice. And then these murdered sailors made their presence felt even on Etruscan soil.

There is in any case a closer connection between Etruscan Agylla and the Greeks, since Agylla was believed to be a Pelasgian or antique Greek foundation, in which the Greek language was spoken. There was a story that when the first Etruscan soldier approached the city which was built to the edges of sheer cliffs on several sides, he shouted to a soldier on Agylla's walls "What is the name of this city?" To this the Agyllan guard answered "Khaire" which is the Greek word for 'Welcome'. And so the Etruscans called the city 'Caere.' If this is true, then the appeal to Delphi is much more understandable, though the mass murder becomes even less so, since now we have a case of Greeks on Greeks. And the institution of games makes more sense, since it was a prescription for a city traditionally Greek.

Quite how these murdered sailors achieved their supernatural effect is obviously beyond our understanding. But we may safely assume two things about Delphi's response: first, that the grand funeral ceremony and the periodic games were an effective antidote to the miasma or curse on the place where the sailors had lain, and to any other effects of the curse. But the magic antidote had to be repeated. Assuming this, we may next assume with equal safety that the effectiveness of the antidote proved that the murdered sailors were heroes in the quite technical sense that they were semi-divine beings. For otherwise the games would not have assuaged the desire made manifest by the curse. From this we can see the significance of Herodotus' account of the sea battle in which these victorious sailors were outnumbered two to one. We forget a little that they had been acting like pirates for the five years since emigrating from Asia Minor to Corsica, but we remember that they alone with the Teans had followed Delphi's counsel in so emigrating. These sailors, in their way, were very like the Christian martyrs whose blood, brutally shed on foreign soil, was sanctifying that soil.

The physical massacre and the paralysis are powerful supernatural events. The grand funeral ceremony, the athletic and equestrian contests are also supernatural in their effect, since they remove or balance the curse. So the games here are a form of magic, and those who speak these days of the magic of the games are more right than they realize. Hamlet senior was murdered and walked as a ghost which required vengeance. But not these murdered sailors. They are placated by the funeral and the games. It may just be that the grand funeral for the sailors involved ritual human sacrifice as Achilles sacrificed twelve young Trojan noblemen at the funeral pyre of Patroclus. But Herodotus certainly does not tell us so. On his account we must suppose the games and funeral ceremony were needed to counteract the curse and that they sufficed.

Rather than the *lex talionis* by which blood is requited by blood, we may even have here magic of precisely and exactly the opposite kind. In vengeance blood calls for blood, but these games provided a magical substitute for the tit-for-tat of retribution, a mimic war and mimic victor acknowledged by all sides and beyond dispute. It was precisely the harmony and regulation of these games and the critical emphasis on not damaging your competitors or opponents which counteracted the curse, an equal and opposite reaction of quite the other kind from retribution. We can bring the thought still more sharply into focus when we compare and contrast the founding and conduct of these Etruscan games with another Italian way of celebrating funerals, gladiatorial contests to the death.

The Romans put on gladiatorial contests to celebrate funerals from the early fifth century BC at least, and there is evidence to suggest that they borrowed the custom from the Etruscans. Pairs of slaves fought to the death before funeral guests, presumably as a form of human sacrifice. In the *Iliad* Achilles slaughters twelve young Trojan noblemen at Patroclus' pyre before presiding over the games in Patroclus' honour. Leaving aside the rank of the Trojan victims, we might suppose that the Greek style of games plus human sacrifice equals gladiatorial combat to the death. But the Greek games as such rigorously and carefully minimized the risk of death to the competitors and this too is as old as the Trojan War. Homer describes the single combat with spears between Ajax and Diomedes at the games for Patroclus which the troops themselves demanded be stopped out of their fear for Ajax. Achilles had specified that the victor would be the first man to draw serious blood from his opponent.

Perhaps the Greek troops at Troy felt a special affection for Ajax or were anxious not to lose one or both men, who were among their best leaders. Yet the spirit of those games for Patroclus is otherwise lofty, generous and magnanimous to losers, as when Achilles quite arbitrarily awards second prize in the chariot race to Eumelus who crashed at the turning post and limped in on foot behind all the other competitors, carrying the remains of his chariot with him. Can we claim that the Greek games were a deliberate contrivance to purify the manners of men and raise them above brutality? In the case of Achilles in his rage they were only partially successful if this was their aim. If it was, the Greeks too may have felt disgust at Achilles' killing of the twelve Trojans, as their Gods are clearly disgusted by his abuse of Hector's corpse. As for gladiators, we feel that watching snuff movies is a hideous moral offence; having people killed for the sake of spectacle is dreadfully wrong. The Greeks may have helped impart that sensibility to us. Many Greeks in the sixth and fifth centuries BC were queasy about sacrificing animals, so it is hard to see how they could have accepted the gladiatorial spectacle. In the fifth century Greek theatre carefully excluded from the stage the killing, though not the dying, of tragic heroes.

If we have to choose between cold-blooded ritual murders in Achilles' manner, gladiatorial contests to the death or the Greek games as ways of celebrating funerals, there is no question which we would choose. We do not know enough about Etruria in the sixth century BC to gauge exactly how the predicament of Agylla and its resolution figured in the intercultural conflict in Italy. But we may, I think, entertain a suspicion that Delphi here was engaged in a self-conscious "civilizing mission", that the God Apollo was teaching the Etruscans a lesson in magnanimity. Whether this is true or not, the Greeks certainly believed that the killing of other people is not a suitable spectacle for humans, even when only play-acted. It is a suitable spectacle for the Gods whose immortality and divine fore-knowledge of our destinies gives them a distinctly different point of view from ours. But the Gods, too, mourn the deaths of their favor-ites on the battlefield. To the Gods, indeed, our human world is *the* spectacle and their watching of it their most characteristic activity. Watching our world is the divine act, the daily pleasure of Olympus. We humans, too, love to be spectators but the real world with its killing is too big for our eyes, too terrifying. We are like Arjuna when Krishna reveals himself as the devouring world in the *Bhaga-vad Gita*. We cannot witness the killing of people with the equanim-ity necessary to spectators, unless we are debased. And so we have devised safer worlds, the games and the theatre, whose events we can bear to witness as spectators. With epic we do taste the power of seeing a whole world and its killing from the point of view of Gods. Here the slayings are rarefied and sufficiently transformed by word and metre.

Let us return to the institution of those Etruscan games described by Herodotus. There is a certain congruence between the circum-stances under which these games came to be held and the nature of games as we have discussed it. The massacre of Greek heroes by Agyllans is compensated not by retribution or human sacrifice or blood-money but by the harmony induced at a repeated ritual on Delphi's terms. In these rituals Greeks and Greek Etruscans were brought together on Etruscan soil and at Etruscan expense, but as competitors and spectators they were all placed on the most strictly equal basis. No doubt Agyllan worthies and representatives of the Greek victims were honoured with seats at the front. They witness or engage in contests in which the damage inflicted on contestants is limited, and in which civility and magnanimity are respected. There is a touch of genius about the arrangement when we consider the gravity of the offence which it expiates. Delphi's *imperium* is exercised with forbearance, positively, even joyfully when we remember that these games were festivals. I do not find it hard to see the influence of Delphi here as a spiritual influence. Even so, I do not think we have yet reached an explanation of why these games could expiate that curse. For this we must turn to considering the athletes in competition.

Here is a possible answer to our question 'how was the curse expiated by these games?' The curse arose when Greek sailors who had won an heroic victory over a fleet twice the size of their own, and who had been taken prisoners, were murdered. The murder of prisoners was contrary to the normal usages of Greek warfare but the offence here was particularly heinous because the victims had just proved themselves great warriors. Victory is a Goddess of the games as well as of warfare, and in the games the achievement of victory is always acknowledged and honoured. In those Etruscan games ordered by Delphi, in which Greeks and Etruscans competed as equals, every event had its winner, determined by the strictest rules and duly honoured. The process, repeated again and again throughout each festival, is a kind of reversal to the doom of the unfortunate sailors, as though every first prize was in effect the belated award of victory to those heroes in whose honour the festival was held. The justice which governed these games undid the injustice which had provoked the curse. But the magical performance had to be repeated indefinitely to keep the curse away.

The ceremony of crowning the victor is an active antidote to the curse. The Greek conception of the games might have arisen just to serve such a placatory and expiatory formula, when the games appeared many centuries earlier. We must take this celebration of the victor very seriously as a ritual of the games. The ritual of the victor is the elevation of one man in the group to a quasi-divine status, for these are the terms in which Pindar, the poet of the Greek games, sings of the winners whose nations, cities and families he celebrates. The elevation of one among the group in ritual, to honour him almost as a God, occurs outside the celebration of victors as well. It seems to be cult practice, at least in southern Italy about 500 BC and in late archaic Crete. In these cases the elevated one has a title 'the *Kouros*'. This, it must be said, is not a very startling title in itself, since it simply means 'young man'. But this same title was ritually accorded to many Gods, Zeus, Dionysus and Apollo among them. And it is, of course, the name given to the most characteristic of Archaic statuary forms, the standing nude young man, arms at side and one foot slightly forward.

The young man is elevated above the rest as the representative to them of the God or hero. He is the object of all eyes. The pose of the *Kouros* statue might represent the young man as he steps forward to receive the crown of victory. The nakedness, the modest dignity, the slight smile which reveals that this is an occasion for joy. And these young men were also warriors, braves in the army or navy. There is a profoundly elegiac tone to the picture of the *Kouros*, like the feelings aroused in Homer's Odysseus by the inglorious death of his youngest companion, Elpenor. This complex of feelings, celebratory, contemplative, elegiac, would have had quite special force in the games of those just dead sailors. We hear a similar tone in Milton's *Lycidas*, Shelley's *Adonais*, Tennyson's *In Memoriam* and perhaps most clearly in A.E. Housman. There is something divine about it, as when Zeus himself grieves for the death of Sarpedon outside the walls of Troy. In those Etruscan games, above all, the juxtaposition of the life on field and track with the deaths which occasioned it must have been most poignant.

The figure of the *Kouros* played an important part in the lives of the survivors of the sea battle and the mass murder. The Greeks were forced to abandon Corsica after the sea battle, and the survivors resettled on the west coast of Italy at Elea, now Velia, south of Naples. Elea was one of the places where there seemed to have been ritual processions which chose one from among their number to represent a God or hero. We may assume this of Elea from a poem composed within the first generation of the resettlement there. In this poem a speeding chariot rider is escorted by maidens to a palace where a Goddess receives him and greets him as follows:

> *O Kouros, companion of deathless charioteers,*
> *These horses who bring you as far as our house,*
> *Welcome! For no evil Fate predestined you*
> *To take this road so far from the path of men,*
> *But Right and Justice.*[3]

When we put these lines with what we know of this people's immediate past, it is hard not to see in the chariot rider's apotheosis another echo of the massacre and its aftermath. Like the murdered sailors, the chariot rider is being induced into a divine order. The Goddess denies that an evil fate has brought him to her. Why should he have thought that it was evil? We can see why he might have thought so, given his people's exceptional sufferings. They had followed Delphi's advice and migrated and it had turned out disastrously. But perhaps, finally, it was all to turn out for the best.

Fine though it is to be a victor at the games, it is finer still to die courageously in war as those sailors died. Greater deaths meet greater destinies, Heraclitus says.[4] Dry souls are wisest and there is no soul drier than the soul of the warrior fighting for his city. The Elean poem and the Agyllan games may usefully be considered as parallel responses to the heroism of the migration, the sea battle and its consequences. The young man who goes to the Goddess in the poem is at one with the heroes whom the games divinize in the form of victorious athletes. The Etruscan games, though they lasted to Herodotus' own time, did not, perhaps, count for much in the history of Greek athletics. But the Elean poem became the foundation of Greek and Western metaphysics. The reality into which the Goddess induced the young man through the poem was the first and remained the clearest account of the Absolute in Greek thought. The author of the poem, Parmenides, was the greatest single philosophical influence on Plato. In this way these events on and off the west coast of Italy between 545 and 500 BC have played a glorious, if largely unknown, part in our own intellectual history.

The Etruscan games of Agylla were not of the first importance in themselves, but we know more about them than we know of other games. These games honoured heroes, men who had achieved metamorphosis into the divine. The games were a ritual enactment of the process of heroization. The heroic struggle to the death was represented by competition among athletes, and the achieving of immortality was represented by the crowning of the victor. On this

---

3. Parmenides, Frag. I, 24–28.
4. Heraclitus, Frag. 25 and 18.

view, to treat winners at the games as semi-divine in their own right would be like mistaking the lead actor in a passion play for the very Christ. Winning at the games symbolized the hero's achievement of immortality but it was not itself the achieving of that immortality except in the limited sense of fame among men. Competing in the Greek games may or may not have prepared the athletes for actual warfare. The matter was much debated in antiquity. But competing and winning in these Etruscan games, at least, most certainly represented the actual fighting and triumph of those sailors.

In fact the institution of the funeral ceremony and the games turned out to be of the very greatest advantage to the citizens of Agylla. It looks as though the power of these ceremonies far exceeded the immediate need to placate the murdered sailors. Agylla hereafter became the single largest burial site in the whole of the Mediterranean basin, the famous *Banditacchia*. It is hard not to see a connection between this signal fact and the events and ceremonies we have discussed. Inversely, the scene of a major pollution, once purified, became the most purified place of all. We know from Herodotus that the rituals in honour of the sailors continued for at least a century. The long-term success of the cemetery gives us a sense of the rituals' power.

2

'RENDER THEREFORE UNTO CAESAR...'

Luke 20:25

This text, with its parallels in Matthew and Mark, is often preached. According to many preachers Christ here acknowledged our obligations to the temporal order, where his questioners had hoped he would outrage the occupying Romans by denying the legality of their taxes. But I note that when Jesus does not encourage default, his questioners are not merely disappointed, they are wonderstruck. The usual reading does not explain that.

Who is there in the temple with Jesus on this occasion? First there are his questioners, 'sitters-in-wait' to translate the Greek term exactly. The high priests and the scribes had publicly questioned Jesus' authority as a teacher earlier in the chapter but Jesus' reply outwitted them. Now they have put their agents into the temple to await Jesus' next appearance. The temple authorities have Jesus under surveillance. When Jesus appears again in the temple, the 'sitters-in-wait' pretend to accept his authority as a teacher and attempt to lure him into a denunciation of the Roman taxes. We may infer that those same high priests and scribes would have been there in the temple to watch closely the outcome of their latest manoeuvre. But there is another presence there in the temple that day, though it is not mentioned until the end of the episode. That presence is the people, whom the temple authorities are anxious to keep on their side. If we take it that the people resented their Roman taxes, then this new manoeuvre of the temple authorities with the 'sitters-in-wait' begins to make sense. It is Morton's fork. Either

Jesus denounces the Roman taxes and is in trouble with the occupying power or he approves the taxes and loses popular support.

In these circumstances, then, Jesus has been asked a very difficult question. But it is much more difficult than I have so far described. In this dialectical contest, the questioners have had any amount of time and expert assistance in the framing of their question. Jesus has neither: he must answer on the spot and without counsel. Furthermore he must, I think, answer briefly, in just a few words. This is the form of dialectical contest called *brachylogia* as against *macrologia*, and brevity is at a premium. Either answer will damage him. Nor can he prevaricate as easily this time as when he turned aside the questioning of his authority as a teacher merely by asking a question of his own. Immediately he must now compose or recall a sufficiently gnomic answer, which both accommodates the Romans and satisfies the anti-Roman populace.

His response, I think, is immediate: "Why do you test me?" This is the question one asks of the Devil. The questioners' pretence that they acknowledge his authority as a teacher he rejects clearly. This rejection must have increased the pressure. He has everyone's full attention. Again without a pause he says "Show me a Roman penny." Now there is a pause but it is hardly a pause which Jesus can exploit to frame his answer. His asking for the coin suggests that he already has his answer, to which the coin is integral. How long would it have taken them to produce a penny? The Romans carried their coins in their mouths. Was it strictly proper to make a show of Roman, or indeed any foreign coinage in the temple. If it was not proper, then Jesus' request was provocative and twisted the tension even higher. "Whose image and inscription does it bear?" The Jews had been commanded by Moses not to make graven images for worship, and they maintained an opposition to representational art more generally. Jesus is being still more provocative by calling this huge cultural gap between Jews and Romans into the open.

The 'sitters-in-wait' give Jesus the answer he clearly expects: "Caesar's." As they spoke they must have been hopeful that he would fall into their trap and denounce the Roman taxes. Why otherwise would he have asked to be shown the penny? As soon as they answer his question, he answers theirs. Whatever his answer meant to his questioners and the listening people, it cannot simply have meant what many preachers take it to mean, that we should observe our duties to the state. This way of taking Jesus' answer would neither have amazed his questioners nor satisfied the people. They must have taken his answer in some other way. Somehow those few words of Jesus perfectly met the case and disposed of the challenge. It is true that Jesus' answer does distinguish sharply between Caesar and God but it was not Caesar's divinity that was immediately in question here, but Caesar's taxes.

Understanding the power of Jesus' answers requires the application of a certain logic to what has been done and said so far in this encounter. But the logic to be applied requires wit of a kind much more common in the ancient world than in our own time. It is a matter of ratios. Because the coin bears the image and inscription of Caesar it belongs to Caesar. All those things which bear the image and inscription of Caesar are the things of Caesar and belong to Caesar. What then are the things of God? The things of God must be all those things which bear the image and inscription of God. For the Hebrews there was one thing above all which bore the image of God and that was man. For so Moses had taught them in the very first verses of the scriptures.[1] So for the very same reason that the penny belongs to Caesar, man belongs to God. But Caesar is a man. Therefore, just as the coin belongs to Caesar, Caesar belongs to the Hebrew God.

The logic of these inferences may seem a little attenuated to the modern reader. Partly this is because we are no longer used to thinking in ratios. One way of describing Jesus' gnomic answer would be to say that it propounds an algebraic equation of four terms of which the last is the unknown X. The four terms are: Caesar, coins, God, and the things of God. The question is: 'What are the things of God?' Jesus' formulation is a riddle. And like the riddle of the Sphinx, the solution to Jesus' riddle is 'Man'. We, on the other hand, have lost interest in riddles. Partly, too, the logical inferences seem thin to us because the notion that people are made in the image and likeness of God is no longer central to our epistemology

1. Genesis 1:26.

in general nor to our natural sciences in particular. Given our limitations in these two respects, it is not difficult to understand how some have misunderstood the exact meaning of their text. And indeed we wonder, on this interpretation, just how long it took for Jesus' audience to see the point. For the penny to drop. And when it had dropped, when the leaders of that congregation by sign or silence gave their assent, just how did Jesus' reply affect the tensions in that chamber?

The 'sitters-in-wait' must have been disappointed. There was nothing in Jesus' answer which they could usefully report to the Romans. The Romans would understand Jesus' answer as properly submissive, and the point of the answer would escape them since they did not believe what the Jews believed about God's creation of man in his own image. In this regard the Roman reading of Jesus' answer would exactly match the usual reading I have already presented: Jesus had acknowledged the Jews' obligation to the temporal order. And the 'sitters-in-wait' must have been doubly disappointed that Jesus had also escaped the other horn of the dilemma in which they had entrapped him. Though they could not explain it effectively to the Romans, Jesus' answer was at once revolutionary and orthodox from the Jewish perspective. By implying that Caesar was himself the creation and possession of Jehovah, Jesus had in eight syllables defined the relation between the Jewish faith and the occupying power. The Romans too belonged to Jehovah.

This aspect of Jesus' intellectual triumph has a more negative and Nietzschean angle. The mere assertion that Jehovah made and owns Caesar, even if explicit, is a very feeble response to the actual fact of foreign occupation. Similarly for those muttering Christians in the *Genealogy of Morals*, their belief in an afterlife in which the slaves will be masters is nothing but the most impotent and cowardly resentment. Contrast this with the claim in Blake's *Marriage of Heaven and Hell*: that because the Jews believed only in their God and cursed all other Gods in his name, so at last the whole world has come to accept their view of God and worship him, for such is the power of faith.[2] In that context, Jesus' defining of the Jewish

2. William Blake, *The Marriage of Heaven and Hell*, pl. 13.

cause in relation to the Roman *imperium* was a sublime example of that same faith.

Those people in the temple would have interpreted Jesus' words in the way that Blake interprets the Bible, not as Nietzsche heard the Christians. If the 'sitters-in-wait' had been very quick they would immediately have answered Jesus: "Yes, but should we pay the taxes to Caesar?" But they made the mistake of trying to understand him and their brief chance was lost. There was amazement in the temple that day at Jesus' dialectical *éclat*. Well, should we pay taxes to Caesar? In fact, this story offers us very little on that question. But the verse is often used to urge and justify some supposed duty to the state, and has smoothed the way for many crimes.

3

THREE SHORT ESSAYS
IN ASTROPHYSIOLOGY

The Man in the Zodiac

To this day there is no wholly plausible explanation, nor yet range of explanations, for the twelve Zodiacal signs. No single set of phenomena has been identified to which the twelve signs correspond in their sequence. Least of all may we see them unambiguously in the stars.[1] On the explanations presently available, the twelve Zodiacal signs were already the result of a hotchpotch of influences by the time of Aratus (c.315 BC–240 BC) and the temples at Esneé and Dendera.[2] But this is to take an unduly pessimistic position. The chances of finding a single persuasive explanation should be much better than this. Our situation is like that of a detective with certain items of information to help him identify his quarry. Suppose X to live in Manchester. This reduces the pool to a few million. Suppose X red haired. This reduces the millions to a few hundred thousand. Each new item of information further reduces the pool which contains X. If there are enough items of information, and they are specific enough, then the pool reduces to a single individual. Similarly with the twelve signs in strict order. It is most unlikely that there are even two sets of phenomena which will fit the series sign

---

1. Louis MacNiece remarks: 'Of the constellations, Leo is the only one who looks like his name.' *Astrology* (London: Aldus Books, 1964), pp. 75–76.

2. Aratus, *Phaenomena* (Cambridge, MA: Loeb Classical Library, 1955), p.1; tr. G. Mair, *Description de I'Egypte*, Vol. J (Bonn: Benedikt Taschen Verlag, 1994), plates 87 & 120.

by sign. Twelve is a huge number of complex items of information, and their being in strict sequence is a further extremely limiting factor. The riddle begs for a solution.

Let us rehearse just one feature of the Zodiacal calendar. The first degree of Cancer is the Summer Solstice in the Northern Hemisphere; the first degree of Capricorn is the Winter Solstice. From Cancer through Sagittarius is the descending half of the year during which the sun moves South; from Capricorn through Gemini is the ascending half of the year during which the sun moves North.

Aratus begins our earliest complete account of the twelve Zodiacal signs from Cancer, but he does not ascribe the signs to parts of the human body.[3] Manilius is the first to do so and he begins from equinoctial Aries at the head.[4] I agree with Manilius that the twelve Zodiacal signs represent the human form. But I say that the signs from Cancer through Sagittarius represent a man's back in descending order; the signs from Capricorn through Gemini represent his front in ascending order. As follows:

FRONT	CROWN	CANCER
GEMINI	HEAD	LEO
TAURUS	NECK	VIRGO
ARIES	THORAX	LIBRA
PISCES	WAIST	SCORPIO
AQUARIUS	LOINS	SAGITTARIUS
CAPRICORN	PERINEUM	BACK

CANCER is the year's zenith, the top of the skull. A crab because the cranium is the most exoskeletal part of the body.

3. Aratus, *Phaenomena*, L. 542–552.
4. Manilius, *Astronomica* 2.446–471, tr. G.P. Goold (Cambridge, MA: Loeb Classical Library, 1977).

LEO is the mane of hair which grows over, or only round the cranium.

VIRGO is the nape of the neck, defenceless and mortally vulnerable.

LIBRA is the scales of the shoulders and arms.

SCORPIO is the vertebrae at the small of the back.

SAGITTARIUS is a backside with legs of its own.

CAPRICORN is the nadir, the anus through which waste is ejected and the scrotum from which new life is generated.

AQUARIUS is the ithyphallic pipe which carries the living stream.

PISCES are the ejaculated spermatozoa.

ARIES is the hairy chest of a ram.

TAURUS is the bull's roaring throat.

GEMINI is a pair of eyes.

CANCER is the cranium again.

The twelve Zodiacal signs symbolize all the parts of a line or band around the torso and head of an adult human male. This line is comparable to the two Great Meridians of the human body in Chinese medicine, the first such lines in the study of acupuncture. As the Zodiac the line represents the human male at the very peak of sexual arousal, and the ejaculated seed is also represented. This ascription of the twelve signs to the parts of the human body differs from the traditional doctrine where Aries represents the crown of the head and Pisces the feet. The traditional theory includes the legs but does not distinguish between the ascending and descending signs. As a result Aries is as far from its adjoining sign Pisces as it can be. The traditional theory applies the signs to the body; the account offered here derives the signs from the body. Here the links between body part and sign themselves explain the choice and order of the twelve Zodiacal signs.

If the Zodiacal signs refer to the parts of a man's body, back and front, then these same parts of a man's body relate to the seasons of the year. The head comprises three summer signs of the Northern Hemisphere; the loins three winter signs; the thorax and waist the equinoctial signs. The male body is a representation of those astronomical movements which generate the seasons. The male body is a microcosm of the particular astronomical conditions experienced on earth, geocentrically considered. Here purely temporal divisions are transformed into the spatial articulations of a body. But we achieve a similar transformation every time we imagine how the seasons of the year correspond to the arctic, temperate and equatorial zones of the earth in space.

Let us consider Capricorn. Capricorn is a very odd sign, comprising the front half of a goat and the rear half of a fish. This unfortunate hybrid is in the act of clambering out of the water onto dry land. All this reflects how the Sun's entry into Capricorn marks at once the moment of the Sun's furthest withdrawal from the Northern Hemisphere and the earliest moment of its return. We call this moment a solstice, a stasis or suspension of the Sun's movement north or south, geocentrically considered. According to Aristotle the Sun's approach to the Northern Hemisphere generates life there, while its withdrawal causes destruction.[5] So Midwinter's Day is at once the fullest triumph of chaos and the beginning of a new order. The Greeks and Romans consecrated Capricorn to Saturn since in this sign the Sun was furthest away as Saturn was the most distant of the planets. The Roman Saturnalia and later Greek Kroniades celebrated this God at Midwinter by making the householders slaves and the slaves their masters and mistresses.[6] In a season of good cheer everything was turned upside down and the Lord of Misrule presided over a ritualized revolution.[7] This is the dissolution represented by the fishtail and the water. The goat's clambering

5. Aristotle, vol. III, 336A–336B, *On Coming-To-Be and Passing Away*, tr. E.S. Forster (London: Loeb Classical Library).

6. Macrobius, *Saturnalia*, VII.

7. R. Guénon, *Fundamental Symbols*, 1995, Cambridge, Quinta Essentia, 1995, pp 101–105.

onto the land is the salvation of the New Year which begins the recovery of a pristine order.

The perineum exhibits this same dissonance and doubleness, the weirdness of the goat fish. The defecatory organ is right next to the generative organs. Here too is an end and a beginning. Worse, the urinary organs are, in part, identical with the generative organs:

> *But Love has pitched his mansion in*
> *The place of excrement.*[8]

The waste of the anus is most dead and foul to us, ultimate dissolution. But the testicles are the source, with the female ovaries, of new life. In both sexes the closeness of the excretory to the reproductive organs is a startling thing. The organs which give us our greatest physical pleasure and the organs which most disgust us are side by side or actually identical. And all this is hidden away as secretly as our bodies allow, in the very depth of our winters. The descending path of the Sun from Cancer to Capricorn is the passage from mouth to anus, while the energies generated in the sexual organs rise up and invigorate the body from below. Those energies enable tumescence; the spurting seed; the hair on the chest; the deep loud voice; and most subtly of all, that gleam in the eye.

The Sun's course through the Zodiacal constellations is often represented by an astronomical circle drawn right round the sky above and below the horizon at an angle to the equator. The Zodiacal constellations above the equator are in the Northern Hemisphere where they are the signs of Spring and Summer. The signs south of the Equator accompany the Sun during the darker half of the Northern Hemisphere's year. The circle of the Sun's journey through the fixed stars bisects the equator at an angle of some 24 degrees; the constellations of Cancer and Capricorn occupy areas of the sky 24 degrees above and 24 degrees below the equator. But because Cancer and Capricorn are traditionally the Solstitial signs and mark the Sun's most extreme movements north and south, these two signs are themselves taken to represent the North and South of the years. The

---

8. W.B. Yeats, "Crazy Jane Talks with the Bishop," from *Words for Music Perhaps*, 1933.

Zodiacal hoop which is actually set at only a slight angle to the equator is now forced onto its edge at right-angles to the equator. In this way the astronomical circle which we call the ecliptic is converted into a meridian. Now the line drawn from the first point of Cancer to the first point of Capricorn represents the pole itself, with the first point of Cancer as North Pole and the first point of Capricorn as South Pole. This pole is then assimilated to the human spine. Similarly the equinoctial signs correspond to the tropics and human thorax and waist.

In this way a geocentric and Northern Hemisphere perspective on the cosmos enables an identification of the Zodiacal signs with the latitudes and of both with the male form. Summer is northern, Spring and Autumn equatorial, Winter is southern. Like the seasonal structure, this polar structure too is found in the male body, as the spine. Since a man's body is connected not only with the seasons but with the latitudes, the Sun's journeys between its Northern and Southern tropics are one basis for understanding human anatomy.

I have used the expression 'geocentric perspective.' We have been concerned here with the relations between the heavenly movements and a man's body. We may think of that body as a microcosmic representation of the particular astral conditions which bear upon the earth on which men live. It is just these astronomical conditions as they affect the earth that shape the human body. So the heliocentric system is much less useful here than the notion of the Sun's moving through its signs. The derivation of the correspondences between the living body and the stars proceeds quite properly and scientifically on the geocentric system as the one applicable in this context of astro-anatomy.

Let us now bisect our solstitial Zodiac through the Equinoxes and not the Solstices. We draw an imaginary line from the first point of Aries, the Spring equinox, to the first point in Libra, the Autumn equinox. If we do the same to our male head and torso we divide it into two halves. The upper half comprises the head with the front of the torso as far as the sternum, and the back to the base of the nape. The classical bust.

According to Porphyry, Homer's Cave of the Nymphs in the

Odyssey has Cancer and Capricorn as its two gates North and South.[9] The Northern gate is the way down for mortals; the Southern gate is for immortals only. We may assume that it is through the Southern gate that Odysseus passes with Athene. René Guénon identified Porphyry's reading of Homer's Cave with Hindu doctrine concerning the light and dark halves of the year, interpreted solstistially.[10] If Porphyry is not anachronistic, then Homer knew the Zodiac as having two halves and as turning on what were traditionally the most northern and the most southern constellations in the Sun's path.

Proportions of Venus

The equinoctial and solstitial readings of the Zodiac both ascribe the signs to parts of the human body. These ascriptions demand methodological justification since scientists now generally dismiss them. Ascribing the star signs to the human body has this much in common with contemporary scientific theory: these ascriptions too are fully expressible mathematically and are quite as exact. So, on the solstitial reading:

Cancer : crown : : Taurus : throat

and

Cancer : Taurus : : crown throat

Euclid developed the theory of ratios and proportions in the fifth book of the Elements. In song the same science is realized in metre, metaphor and the musical intervals; Platonic astronomy turns on the mathematics of the diatonic scale;[11] again, according to Plato, fire is to air as air is to water as water is to earth.[12] Anatomy and sculpture are also based on the proportionate relations between all the parts and wholes of animal bodies, as shown in the works of

9. Porphyry, *Concerning the Cave of the Nymphs*, tr. T. Taylor, in *Thomas Taylor the Platonist*, ed. K. Raine & G.H. Mills (London: Routledge & Kegan Paul, 1969), p.309.

10. R. Guénon, *Fundamental Symbols*, op. cit., p. 159.

11. Plato, *Republic*, 617B.

12. Plato, *Timaeus*, 32B.

Polycleitus. Ancient science and art exhibit a general preference for understanding in terms of proportion.

The case of metaphor is most striking. *If brains were dynamite, yours wouldn't blow your hat off* identifies the relation between brain and hat with that between, say, mine and dirt. *Stephen Dedalus walked the streets of Dublin like the old moon looking at the young earth* identifies the relation between Dedalus and Dublin with that between old moon and young earth. Literature and wit too are often mathematical arts by which we come to understand the unknown, your brain power, Stephen's mood, by solving an equation in which all the other terms and the ratio are known to us.

The same science of proportions accommodates theology too. Take as an example an ancient rite of the goddess Athene. In Homer's *Iliad* the Trojan noblewomen present a robe to a statue of Athene as they pray that the goddess defend the walls of Troy against attack.[13] In the yearly festival of the Panathenaea the Athenians also presented a robe to a statue of the goddess. It seems that the robe of the goddess is the wall of the city metaphorically. The Athenians began the weaving of their robe nine months before its presentation to the Goddess. The weaving began at the Khalkeia, a festival which celebrated group marriages. From this point of view the robe is a symbol of the human body which is nine months in the weaving or gestation. For just as the robe clothes the body, so the body clothes the soul with the unfamiliar tunic of our flesh.[14]

$$\text{Soul/body} = \text{body/robe} = \text{robe/walls}$$

With these successive investitures we have a parallel to the notes of the musical scale, which can also constitute a series in which a note is linked to the one before it and the one after it by the same ratio. One ratio generates the intervals of a regular gradation along a single continuum. In the case of the musical notes, the continuum is pitch. In the case of Athene, successive sheaths. In the case of the four elements, it is their relative density. But a single ratio may also

13. *Iliad* 6.286–311.
14. Empedocles, Frag. 126; cf. Frag. 120, and Homer's account of Athene and Odysseus at the Cave of the Nymphs on Ithaca, and Porphyry's account of both.

generate a number of terms discontinuously. So instead of the same ratio in the intervals of the terms in a series along one continuum:

$$a/b = b/c = c/d = d/e = e/f...$$

the same ratio may represent the intervals of terms discontinuously across two or more different continua. In this way we can apply the one ratio or relation to connect things of quite different kinds, not merely the terms in one continuous range but the terms in two quite different ranges. This is what is happening with the Zodiacal identifications with parts of the human body.

Take another astrophysiological example, the name Venus. The word 'Venus' names a planet and also the Roman goddess of sexual love. The word 'Aphrodite' did the same for the Greeks. The goddess and the planet have the same name. The goddess of love stands over copulation on the pubic mound which bears her name.[15] The planet is the Evening Star which stands over the Sun's entry into the Western darkness. The Sun is the phallus of the Sky God which charges like a chariot into Night's palace. The delicate limbs of love are as full and as pink as the red sky of evening. Venus the planet stands in the same relation to the transition from day to night as Venus the goddess of love stands to the sexual act of male and female. This is why the planet and the goddess of love have the same name. The name is the key to a complex teaching which binds the phenomenon of dusk to animal copulation by virtue of a single ratio or pattern in two different dimensions. The evening sky and the act of love are identifiable.

Day/night = male/female

The word Venus is the clue. Once the thought of comparing day and night with male and female crosses the mind, the discovery of the correspondences continues indefinitely. So day is male, night is female. The galaxy is the milk of night's breasts. The moon measures her menstrual cycle. Through her Western doors the rounded phallus of the sky god enters his wife; in the womb of night the child

---

15. In females the *mons pubis* is sometimes called the *mons Veneris* (mound of Venus).

is conceived and gestates; through her Eastern doors the rounded head of the sky god is born from his mother. There too Venus stands as Morning Star to aid this other passage.

Let us assume for the moment the equivalence between the heavenly movements and animal reproduction. What follows? We might say that the equivalence arises because animals on earth are formed after the pattern of the astral events which condition their existence under the sky. The microcosmic mortal creature reproduces itself in ways which copy the unions and divisions of day and night under which it lives. From a materialist point of view this has a certain appeal: the gross movements of the heavens determine and dominate the puny formations of the animals under them. Or we may prefer the ancient Greek cosmogonists who placed love at the very first beginning of things.[16] In their view, the heavens formed themselves around Love. In this duplication of a single ratio between day and night and between male and female, it seems that neither the astronomical nor the sexological can be given precedence over the other.

We may express the ratio in an indefinitely long and arbitrary sequence as follows: sun/phallus = milky way/milk = moon/menstrual cycle = planet Venus/Goddess of love, and so on. It was precisely the noticing, developing and representation of such patterns which sustained the Greek and Roman theologians. The Greeks thought of order, cosmos, as the systematic repetition of a single pattern. The pattern is repeated uniformly in a continuous series, like the musical notes or the elements, or it is repeated in two quite different and discontinuous dimensions, as in the evening sky and the sexual act. The rationalizing bent of the ancient mind could reach for profound connections between things in ways which we have lost, for all that the musical series is as well known to us as it was to them. Certainly, the application of the one ratio discontinuously and between dimensions is a technique unknown in our sciences now.

Imagine you are standing at some point on the Equator. The Sun will be directly overhead this point at midday at the Equinoxes. Imagine, too, that you are looking West to the Western horizon, and that you have carefully marked in times past the most southerly

16. For example, Parmenides, Frag. 13.

point just touched by the Sun's orb as it sinks below the horizon at the Southern Solstice. You have also marked the most northerly point at the Northern Solstice, and the point where the centre of the Sun's orb sinks below the horizon at the Equinoxes. Imagine now that these three points mark the threshold of a great doorway reaching up to Heaven. Beginning from the furthest point South touched by the Sun, draw a line straight up into the sky. This line is the southern doorpost of the doorway. From the farthest point North do the same to make the northern doorpost. The threshold of the doorway is the section of the Western horizon between the terrestrial Tropics; and the lintel overhead is the corresponding arc of the celestial meridian between the celestial Tropics.

Imagine now that this doorway in the Western sky is filled by a pair of great doors, as high as the Heaven. The door on the left has as its doorpost the line drawn straight up from the southernmost point. The door on the right hangs from an equivalent post in the North. The junction formed when the two doors are closed together is the line from the terrestrial Equator to the celestial Equator. We may imagine that during the six months the Sun is south of the Equator, the door on the left is open. During the six months the Sun is north of the Equator, the door on the right is open. At the Equinoxes both doors are open. Or perhaps they are both shut then and through the tiny aperture between them the Sun passes.

We have imagined the doorway as based on the section of the Western horizon between the extreme points of the Sun's southerly and northerly courses. These points are determined by the eye alone. The same is true of the Sun's risings over the Eastern horizon. At sunset and sunrise we can mark most easily the Sun's courses against the earth. But the doorway we have constructed with its doors may be said to stand at every point along the Sun's journey, though the exact location of its doorposts and doors are indeterminable by the eye except at setting and rising. On every meridian, on every line of longitude drawn round the globe through the poles, we may theoretically mark off the section between the Tropics to serve as the threshold, and the corresponding section of the celestial line of longitude to serve as lintel. In this way we may think of the Sun as passing through the doorway at every point on its journey.

When the Sun sinks in the West, we think of it as entering through the doorway; when the Sun rises in the East, we think of it as leaving through the doorway. But it is just passing through the doorway at every moment and may equally well be imagined as entering or as leaving or as doing both simultaneously at every instant.

So far we have considered the doorway only in respect of the Sun's daily journey from East to West, by which it completes an entire circuit of the earth every day and night. But the Sun also moves against the fixed stars, relative to which its position changes as they all revolve around the earth. In relation to these fixed stars, the Sun fails to keep pace with them by a little less than one degree a day, and it takes a whole year to complete its retrograde circuit round them all. So while the passage of the Sun through the door-way on its daily circuit is the passage of a point between limits vastly wider than itself, the passage of the Sun through the doorway on its yearly circuit completely spans the distance between the limits of the doorposts twice. And though it is paradoxical it is quite proper to speak of the Sun's yearly journey through the fixed stars as a passage from West to East. If we imagine for a moment the fixed stars actually stopped in the sky but the Sun continuing to move in its usual relation to them, then indeed the Sun would slowly move across the sky from West to East, taking six months in one continuous day before disappearing for six months completely. From this point of view the Sun passes through the doors of the doorway going from West to East, just as Apollo is represented in his chariot emerging from the Eastern pediment of his temple at Delphi, above the doorway and double doors of his temple.

This doorway is a symbol of that doorway we have been cutting into the illimitable sky over the last paragraphs. But it is still some conceptual distance from Apollo's temple at Delphi to the movements of the Sun. Building the Sun's doorway into the walls of a temple at once removes the ambiguity between entering and leaving which was a feature of the doorway by itself. On the other hand the pediment of the emerging Apollo is appreciated typically by someone entering the temple. Leaving the temple, one would be turned away from it. The God's emergence balances the worshipper's entrance. The doorway in the sky was determined entirely by the

Sun's movements and the horizon. They were the only material phenomena in an otherwise undifferentiated and limitless expanse. The temple is the solidification of this empty space, which is limited in this representation by the ends of the Eastern wall in which the doorway is set. We may imagine the Sun's journey through space not as the passage of a solid body through a vast, dark void but as the penetration through what is dense and heavy by something extremely light and mobile. In this symbolism the interstellar spaces are assimilated to earth and the passages of Sun, Moon and planets to the tunnels and chambers in a labyrinthine building, say, or a system of underground caves.[17]

In these ways and with these qualifications the doors of Apollo's temple may be compared to the doors of the Sun, and the temple itself may be compared to the cosmos, geocentrically considered. But it is a truism that where temple and cosmos are analogous to each other both will also be analogous to the human body.[18] The cosmos, the temple and the human body are the three primary houses of the spirit. To what in human anatomy do the doors of the temple correspond? The answer is clearly the female *labia majora*. The name Delphi was closely related to the Greek word for womb, *delphys*, and here too was the navel stone, the *omphalos*, which marked the first point of creation.

This account of the doorway began by constructing it on the Western horizon, after marking the Sun's settings. To think of the Sun's journey through the doorway as from East to West is less comprehensive than to think of the movement as from West to East. But at sunset particularly, Venus often appears in great glory on her mount and even the Sun is afraid of her. This Venus is Justice, who measures the Sun's courses. No longer the laughter-loving Goddess of Homer, now she is much-punishing[19] and the agents of her justice are the Furies formed at her birth.[20]

17. For example, Plato, *Phaedo* 111–130.
18. See for example A. Coomaraswamy's essay, "An Indian Temple: The Kandarya Mahadeo" in *Selected Papers Vol.1: Traditional Art & Symbolism*, ed. R. Lipsey.
19. Parmenides, Frag. 1.
20. Heracleitus, Frag. 94.

The Human Head and Face

First, then, the gods, imitating the spherical shape of the universe, enclosed the two divine courses in a spherical body, that, namely which we now term the head.[21]

In Plato's *Timaeus* the gods who make the human head are the stars and planets, to whom the Creator gave the task of creating mortal creatures. The Creator could not accomplish this task himself since anything which the Creator made would last forever. The Creator made the Heavens and the Heavens made us.

The human head is the prime creation in the mortal realm because it most closely follows the pattern of the cosmos. For the purposes of Plato's analysis, the pattern of the cosmos has been founded on two related but distinct phenomena, geocentrically considered: the rotation of the fixed stars and the varying rotations of the planets. Plato calls the rotation of the fixed stars the course or circuit of the Same, and the rotations of the planets, all taken together, the circuit of the Different.[22] Clearly the rotation of the fixed stars, including the circumpolar stars, generates a sphere, and this is the model or pattern of the human head.

But Plato supposes that both the divine circuits are found in the human head, not just the circuit of the Same. Somehow that other circuit which comprises all the motions of the planets in contradistinction to the motion of the fixed stars, somehow this circuit too is bound into the human head. Plato transposes the cosmic motions into a metaphor of human thinking. When the motions of our thinking correspond to the heavenly motions, then we can see what is the same and what is different accurately. But when the motions of our thinking are disrupted, then we lose the capacity for rational judgement.[23] So disrupted can the interior motions become that they are the very reverse of the proper motions. Then everything appears to the judgement as if it were upside down and left to right. This is what the flood of experiences does to us while we are growing

21. Plato, *Timaeus*, 44D.
22. Ibid., 35.
23. Ibid., 89E–90D.

up, and it is only with maturity that the real circuits of the soul can reassert themselves and return us to a harmonious and rational state of mind. In animals this disruption of the proper circuits is not temporary but permanent, and this is reflected in elongations and other distortions in the sphericity of their skulls.

> The race of wild pedestrian animals, again, came from those who had no philosophy in any of their thoughts, and never considered at all about the nature of the heavens, because they had ceased to use the courses of the head... In consequence of these habits of theirs they had their front legs and their heads resting upon the earth to which they were drawn by affinity, and the crowns of theirs heads were elongated and of all sorts of shapes, into which the courses of their souls were crushed by reason of disuse.[24]

Leaving aside comparative cranial morphology, I find it hard to think of my mind or thoughts as moving like the fixed stars and planets in their courses. Plato makes clear that this is a case of 'use it or lose it.'

Human beings who do not practise theoretical astronomy, who do not consciously exercise their spherical mental motions, will be reborn as quadrupeds. Physical astronomers who gape at the actual stars without working out their motions from first principles are reborn as birds.[25] Their heads are still round but on thickish necks and rather small, we are left to infer, and they have wings. But they are also, of course, still bipeds.

Plato here is a philosophical Aristophanes. But the point remains that there is little serious evidence for assimilating our minds and thoughts to the cosmic motions. Though the rotation of the fixed stars provides the model of sphericity after which the human head is made, we have not discovered any link between that head and the circuits of the planets. But there is one feature of the human head which may matter here. In the Myth of Er Plato represents the planetary motions as like the rims of several bowls nesting inside each

24. Plato, *Timaeus*, 91E.
25. Ibid., 91D.

other.[26] These rims form a kind of plane surface like the whorl of a spindle, through the centre of which a shaft or pole passes. The same idea is conveyed by the spinning surface of Homer's Charybdis.[27] The crux is that the motions of the planets, including Sun and Moon, are all unidirectional and they all fall within a narrow belt between Tropics like those of the Sun. The planets rarely move more than 26 degrees north or south of the Equator. From this point of view, the Earth stands in relation to the planets as Saturn to its rings.

If we apply this schema to the human head, we draw a band around the middle of the head, the band's width corresponding proportionately to the tropic band around the earth. This band, it seems to me, would cover the eyes and ears like a blindfold. So the locations of the organs of seeing and hearing in the human head correspond to the location of the planetary tropics in relation to the whole earth. Seeing and hearing are, for Plato, the best of all our senses because they are connected to the heavens.[28] Sight has been given us to see the heavens, whose motions stimulate us to conceive of numbers.[29] From the study of numbers comes philosophy, the best gift of God to man. As for hearing it is made to hear the voice. The voice provides rational speech and singing. Singing employs those intervals which organize the planetary motions, so that listening to music helps to re-establish the planetary motions in our own heads. In this way, though music is not connected directly to the heavens, it is organized by the very same principles which organize the planetary motions, and so is cognate with those motions. There is then, a certain aptness in the placing of these two senses within the area cut out by the motions of the planets. They are the divine senses, the binding of the divine circuit of the Different in our heads.

Select any point on the surface of a sphere. Mark the point diametrically opposite to it on the other side of the sphere. Through

26. Plato, *Republic*, 616c–617b.
27. *Odyssey*, 12. On this comparison and its astrological symbolism, see R. Sworder, *Homer on Immortality in Science and Religion in Archaic Greece* (San Rafael, CA: Sophia Perennis, 2008), pp. 45–49.
28. Plato, *Timaeus*, 47.
29. Plato, *Epinomis* 978; *Timaeus*, 47a–b.

these two points draw two great circles round the sphere at right angles to each other. The sphere now looks like an orange which has been cut into four equal segments and reassembled. Now draw a third great circle equidistant from the two points at which the first two circles crossed and at right angles to those circles. We now have three interlocking circles, each of which is at right angles to the other two, so this figure has much in common with the three dimensional cross.

Applied to the cosmos, the selected point is the celestial North Pole; the point opposite is the celestial South Pole; the first two great circles are two celestial meridians at right angles to each other; the third great circle is the celestial Equator. The same account holds, *mutatis mutandis*, if we apply our sphere to the earth. Applied to the head, the selected point is the fontanelle; the point opposite is the opening to the throat; of the first two great circles, one passes through the fontanelle and the ears, while the other passes through the fontanelle and along the nose; the third great circle passes through the eyes and ears. Of course on this view, strictly, we should have one eye at the front of our heads and one at the back. But, as Plato points out, the gods who made us felt that we needed a distinct forward direction and for this reason shifted all sight to the front and made the human face.[30]

The face is the epitome of the head. The head in all its aspects is more than our seeing can grasp at once. We do not see in the round but from two points on its circumference. The face represents the beauty of the head as seen from the limitation of a narrow point of view. The Sun, Moon and planets shine from our eyes. The eyes move freely in contrast to the face as the planets move variously against the background of the fixed stars. The hairline and the line between the closed lips suggest the arctic and antarctic circles. The point of the chin is a projection of the head's South Pole, to sustain the face's presentation of the head in its entirety. Even the furrows of a worried brow suggest an astronomer's lines of latitude round the Northern Hemisphere. When we look into the face of another person, we are seeing the cosmos as a mortal animal like ourselves.

30. Plato, *Timaeus*, 45A.

The cosmos, too, is a living animal but an everlasting one, and much too big and too complex for us to see with our eyes and know.

Is it true that the head, the face and the human reproductive systems are homologous with the movements of the stars and planets, viewed geocentrically? This is a question in morphology, of the same kind as questions concerning the relations between comparable organs in animals or in plants. In our times morphological studies of animals often proceed on the hypothesis that animals evolve from each other, while Plato supposed that they all descended from the human, becoming increasingly many-legged until they form into snakes and eventually disappear into the sea as fish.[31] Compared to seeing the differences between kinds of animals, the shift from studying the stars to seeing comparable formations in the human is enormous. But there is a certain intuitive rightness in Plato's notion that we are in this way microcosmic representations of the whole, and the physical similarities between the Sun's doors and the female doors, between the human face and the solar system, are immediately engaging, even if *outré*.

Such a physical similarity cannot be claimed in the case of the Zodiac's relation to a man's head and torso. Seeing the seasons of the year as patterned in the same way as the male frame takes more than just a liberated morphological imagination. But even here the claim stands on its own terms. It is simply and strictly a scientific claim even by contemporary uses of the term science. Many, no doubt, would argue that these macrocosmic analogies to the human are bad science, but they would not, I think, dispute that they were scientific hypotheses. Certainly they are not religious or spiritual claims. Plato may have fantasized as to how these correspondences occur in a creation myth, but even in the myth it is the stars and planets which determine the human form. Even here there is nothing in play beyond what is strictly observable.

From a certain point of view, it is quite surprising that this way of

31. Plato, *Timaeus*, 91.

reading the Zodiacal signs, these ways of understanding the human head and reproductive system, are not much better known, in outline if not in detail. After all, they make no claims on faith, they analyze observable data according to known methods, and they provide explanations of phenomena which are peculiarly dear to us. Furthermore, these ways of reading ourselves are enshrined in traditional forms still in vogue among us. But the only explanations current concerning the human complex seem to be socio-biological or neo-Darwinist. Reasons for this oversight are not hard to find. Part of our pride in ourselves comes from our having outstripped our ancestors in our knowledge of the cosmos. Our competitiveness insists that the Einsteinian theory superseded the Newtonian, and the Newtonian superseded the Ptolemaic. We would do much better to suppose that the Ptolemaic system provides us with an adequate account of the universe *geocentrically considered*; the Newtonian provides the heliocentric account; and the Einsteinian the relativist account. We need all these accounts but the geocentric most of all, because this is the one which tells us most of how we ourselves are shaped.

But even if we had retained a lively picture of the geocentric cosmos, would we, then, have infallibly identified the forms of that cosmos with those of the human body? Not, I think, if we were empiricists of the Enlightenment. Even though all the data necessary to these identifications are empirical, and the method is a form of morphological analysis, even so modern empiricism could not entertain these identifications. In the first place they are not quantifiable in the requisite manner. The determination of the identity between ratios in two different dimensions, the astronomical and the zoological in this case, is not a matter of measurement. No imaginable meter could ever compute it. Secondly, the modern empiricist will argue that no physical explanation has yet been offered of how exactly the movements of the geocentric cosmos come to form the human body after their own pattern or vice versa. No evidence has been advanced even to indicate such a causal link. The identifications turn, in fact, upon an absurd and antiquated aetiology by which cause is to effect as original to image. The human body images the stars and planets or the other way round.

But in modern empiricism cause and effect are merely events bound to each other more or less invariably.

These objections have some weight but they are not conclusive. There is nothing unscientific about the notion that certain physical features of the human being parallel features of the planets and stars viewed geocentrically. We can easily imagine data which would confirm or contradict such an hypothesis. If we were to find life forms elsewhere in space which were more or less identical to the human on planets utterly unlike our own macrocosmically, or if we were to find life on planets like our own but no life forms like ours in these respects, either of these discoveries would contradict the hypothesis developed in this essay. But until that time we must, I think, admit most of the claims of this essay into the ranks of scientifically sound empirical hypotheses.

A low rank, but at least it is respectable by the stern standards of modern empiricism. For the ancients, of course, these identifications of cosmic with human formations were much more than mere so-far-untestable possibilities. They were the observable facts which grounded their understanding. It is just here that we can examine more closely the differences between our empiricism and theirs. The ancients admitted many more analogies than we do and founded their understanding on them. Neither we nor the ancients have moved beyond the observable data. So how are we to judge between these two empiricisms?

4

THE PORTLAND VASE

Since the rediscovery some centuries ago of the Portland or Bar-
berini Vase, the Vase has been interpreted in more than a score of
different ways. This multitude of conflicting interpretations shows
that no early one has yet commanded a universal assent and I see no
reason to suppose that the latest ones will succeed any better. Yet the
figures on the Vase are clear and perfect and they are not, so far as
we know, part of some larger design but self contained. How then
have they failed of a satisfactory interpretation by the antiquarians
of generations? Perhaps the answer is that the Vase is not meant to
be interpreted. By this I do not mean that its design has no meaning, is merely decorative, but that its meaning is deliberately concealed by its designer, is veiled as much as it is revealed by the
figures that compose it. It is not quite so strange that scholars of
mythology and historians of art should fail to find a certain interpretation if the expertise of such people is not quite the expertise of
those for whose delight the Vase was created. It may be that neither
brains nor erudition but intellect is needed here. The notion that
there are some truths reserved for a few, which are not for the many,
is the principle of esoteric religion. The art is to transmit these
truths effectively across the ages in full public view.

The Vase has two compartments[1] in each of which there are three
figures if we ignore for the moment the Cupid in the second. The
figures are similarly arranged in the two compartments: in each
there is a female figure at the centre and two outer figures looking

---

1. The two sides of the Vase are reproduced here in a line drawing of the two
compartments executed by M. O. Miller in D. E. L. Haynes, *The Portland Vase* (London: British Museum Publications, 1975). I have transposed the two compartments
from the order in which Ms Miller represents them.

inwards. This similarity of organization invites the viewer
to compare the two compartments with one another. Take
if you will the three figures in
the first compartment in their
order from left to right and
mentally superimpose them
on the three figures in the second compartment in the same
order. To do this with the Vase
alone one would need to know
the figures of the first compartment by heart. Once the
two sets of figures are so
related there is obviously some
congruence: the seated youth
(A) in the first compartment is
very like the standing youth of
the second (D) on whom he is
now superimposed. Let us
suppose that these are in fact
two versions of the same
youth and that their similarity
of appearance and their places
on the left of the two compartments are in-tended to make
us compare the two compartments by some such mental
superimposition as I have described. Like the Greeks and
Romans we read from left to
right and by making use of
this habit the designer of the
Vase makes clearest at the
beginning, on the left, how the
Vase is to be read. If the two

youths (A and D) are the same youth in different poses, what of the two central female figures? The central female figure in the second compartment has a Cupid flying over her head and a serpent in her lap. This serpent has led some interpreters to suppose her to be Thetis, but female figures over whom a Cupid flies are usually Venus, Cupid's mother. The most famous example is Botticelli's *Primavera*.

Let us suppose that the central figure of the second compartment is Venus and that Cupid is there partly for the purpose of showing that she is Venus. What of her counterpart in the first compartment? If the two young males are the same person may not the two central females also be the same person? Let us suppose that the reclining figure (B) is the same person as Venus with Cupid (E). Both are Venus at different phases just as both the male figures on the left are the same young man at different phases. But when we look to the figures on the right of the two compartments we have a problem, for the seated draped female (C) of the first compartment cannot by any imagining be the same person as the standing bearded nude male (F) of the second. This stumbling block in the way of our procedure may seem insuperable and to cast doubt on our achievements so far. But I do not think it does. The identification under a single description of the two incongruent figures on the right is not only possible but most elegant and attractive.

In the first compartment we see a seated draped young male on the left, a similarly posed and attired female on the right and a reclining Venus in the middle. The easiest way of reading this is to suppose it a kind of hieroglyphic sentence in which the two terms related are at the beginning and the end and the term of their relation in the middle. Venus is the Goddess of Love, so let us suppose that the term of their relation is love. Then the first compartment says that the young man on the left loves the woman on the right and reflexively that the woman on the right loves the young man on the left. If we now look at the second compartment we see once again the two terms of the extremes related by the term in the middle and read that the young man on the left loves the bearded man on the right and vice versa. If we now compare the poses of Venus in the two compartments we are struck at once by her languor in the first and alertness in the second. These poses signify the intensity of the love in each case. So the love between the young man and the woman is less intense than the love between the young man and the older man. A closer look at the older man on the right of the second compartment shows that he has adopted a characteristic pose: head on hand he looks like a thinker. An older man who is a thinker, loving and beloved of a younger man, is a Platonic philosopher. So the first compartment represents love between man and woman, the second love between student and teacher in the Platonic tradition; the two compartments of the Portland Vase represent Profane and Sacred Love. The seated draped female (C) and the standing nude bearded male (F) are identical under this description: they are both lovers and beloved of the young man.

Now let us look at the first compartment in detail on the assumption that it is a representation of Profane Love as a Platonist would imagine it. In looking at it we must give special attention to those features of the first compartment by which it differs from the second, since it is by means of these features that the designer makes clear just what he understands by Profane Love in contrast to Sacred Love. The most noticeable feature of the first compartment is the rocky outcrop on which the figures are placed. These rocks do not appear in the second compartment and their purpose here is clear: they symbolize the earthy, earthly nature of Profane Love. We notice also that the seated woman on the right is on a rock separated from the rock on which the young man and Venus are placed and we may suppose this to signify that the relationship of Profane Love prevents or hinders a complete communion between man and woman, that the very bodies by which such love is consummated are at the same time barriers or obstacles to union. The rocks then symbolize the materiality and unbridgeable privacy of our corporeal natures. We note next that in contrast to the figures on the left and right of the second compartment the young man and woman at the extremes of the first are draped with robes. We are to think of the young man and woman in their physical aspect since the robe, after Empedocles,[2] is a symbol of a corporeal nature. And lastly, to

---

2. Empedocles, Frag. 126.

make the same point a third time, we notice the peculiar pose of the two outermost figures, their bodies turned away from each other, their heads looking back over their shoulders towards each other. The point made by the young man's and woman's bodies being turned away from each other is, I think, the same as that made by the separation of the rocks. Even though the subject of this compartment is Profane Love, sexual love, the designer has turned the bodies of the man and woman away from each other to signify the inadequacy of such love, or at least the impossibility of achieving the fullest communion by means of it.

Now the reclining Venus in the middle of the first compartment. Her legs and feet are towards the young man, and her feet are crossed. Her head is furthest from the young man, averted from him and from the woman on the right, looking dreamily at the ground beyond her, shielded from the young man's gaze by an upraised arm. The crossed feet, the averted eyes, the shielding arm all signify that in this compartment the young man, though close to Venus, is also a long way from knowing her fully. The turning of her legs and body towards the young man and her head away from him suggests that the young man knows the physical but not the spiritual or intellectual Venus. The languor of her pose is at once erotic and indifferent. The dreaminess of her expression and her careless holding of a torch indicate that the scene is an evening or night one and the first and most obvious meaning of the torch is that it represents the Evening Star, at its lowest, just before full night. But the torch so carelessly held upside down is also a phallic symbol, from its position here symbolic of a flaccid penis; head pointing towards the ground it is another ironic comment on the inadequacy of sexual love. At Venus' feet on the ground, resting against a rock as though to show us better what it is, is an object very variously interpreted by critics of the Vase. There is no need to introduce here new elements into the composition. This rectilinear object is the abacus or capital of the pilaster to the left of the youth in the first compartment. The rectilinear cavity at its centre is a means perhaps by which it was affixed to the pilaster. Its being cast down here not only contrasts with its elevation to the left of the young man; it corresponds also to the inverted torch in Venus' hand.

Two more general features to conclude this account of the first compartment. First, the scene has a weightiness about it. Everything here seems weighed down, languorous, oppressed. All the figures are sitting or reclining. The young man and Venus support themselves on an elbow; the young woman on the right on her arm and hand and with a staff; the torch hangs downward from Venus' nerveless hand; there is no flying Cupid; the stratification of the heavy rocks on which the figures are posed stresses the horizontal; even the tree, whatever it is, bows down more in this compartment than do the trees in the other. Everything is nerveless, needs lifting up, requires support. All this symbolizes night and the heavy folds of matter as the Platonist conceives it. Secondly, in comparison to the second compartment, the figures here are separated from one another, their limbs do not touch or overlap but there is a space around each of the three, no mean achievement when we consider the narrowness of the space available on the Vase. This separateness signifies once more the insularity of a corporeal existence.

Now for the detail of the second compartment. But first my reason for calling it the second. It seems to me that the tree to the right of the bearded man who is on the right of my second compartment and the pilaster to the left of the youth seated on the left of my first compartment create together a barrier which makes it rather difficult to read from the bearded man to the seated youth or vice versa. And of course there is between the two compartments at this point the base of a handle and dependent from it a head or mask. There is another handle and head at the point between the seated woman on the right of the first compartment and the young man standing on the left of the second. But here between these two figures and beneath the dependent head there is a shrub or tree, on the left almost touching the seated woman's knee and on the right emerging from the column on the extreme left hand side of the second compartment. This plant establishes a continuity between the two compartments at this point while the absence of any such device on the other side of the Vase and the barrier described above indicate that this is where the sequence begins and ends. If this is so and the policy of reading from left to right is correct, then we are to think of the young man as having been seated in the first compartment and as now standing when we come to the second. What happens in the first compartment, when we reach the second, we are to think of as having happened before the event represented in the second. And so my reason for calling them the first and second compartments.

The first object we meet on turning to the second compartment is a building, either an arch or perhaps part of a larger structure. It is past or through this building that we may presume the young man to have come and we note that this building has its parallel in place in the first compartment, the pilaster to the left of the seated young man. In the second compartment the building's architecture is not unlike that of a temple though it need not be. Nonetheless beyond this building, to the right of it in the second compartment, is Venus with Cupid. So it may well be a temple. The placing of a temple at this transitional point between the two compartments, after the first and as part of the second, would make clear that the event represented in the first compartment is literally profane, that is, in front of the temple, whereas what happens in the second, in which the building appears, is not. At the same time the presence in the first compartment of the pilaster and of the Goddess herself would show that this scene too is connected with the divine, albeit to a lesser degree as the smallness of the column and the Goddess's pose make clear. We may say then that the first compartment illustrates the lesser, the second the greater Mysteries of Venus.

The youth standing on the left of the second compartment is nude though he is holding a robe, part of which is resting or caught on a corner at the base of a column of the building. Since in the first compartment he was wearing a robe, the inference is that he has just now taken it off. But he is still holding it. Likewise the bearded man on the right is nude but has wrapped a robe round behind his back as though deliberately to expose himself. That these two figures should be more nude than their counterparts in the first compartment shows that their love is less physical, more spiritual.[3] That they should not have divested themselves entirely shows that they are still as it were in the body, that the love represented here is a relationship between human beings in the world. Their bodily exposure to each

3. Cf. Titian, *Sacred and Profane Love*.

other, full frontal nudity, demonstrates the completeness of their communion, and their standing poses suggest that they are not now weighed down by matter but self subsistent, autonomous and free in the sphere of intellect. The young man's energetic nudity and the older man's contemplation of it make it hard to resist the memory of Socrates gazing on the young Charmides in the Palaestra. Certainly it is a daytime scene. By the flying Cupid, the young man has been led to where he is now, to where Venus looks him in the face and grasps his arm with the same right arm by which previously she had concealed herself from him. The arch and the catching of his robe signify his arrival into the inner temple. They are sexual symbols to represent his transcending of the sexual.

We come now to the most awful and seemingly most anomalous symbol in the entire composition-the rearing serpent on Venus' lap. This serpent is quite unlike anything else in the piece. We may wonder at the abacus, if that is what it is, in the first compartment or at the staff with which the seated woman on the right supports herself, but they do not seem out of place. But the serpent introduces a whole new order, the only non-personal animal in the design and not a creature, one would think, to have on one's lap. And our attention is directed to it by the composition. It is placed in the very centre of the second compartment and the strong sinuous curve of its back is repeated nowhere else. It is obviously of quite central importance. And what would Venus be doing with such a creature? All this has led some critics of the Vase to base their accounts of it on this creature and to suppose that despite the presence of Cupid over the female figure's head, she cannot be Venus at all. Arguing that the form of the serpent makes clear that it is a special kind of serpent, a sea serpent, they suppose the lady on whose lap it is to be Thetis and the serpent her pet or a token of her transformations, placed here to show that this is indeed who she is. Certainly this way of explaining the serpent would seem to account for its presence rather better than my own interpretation of the Vase to this point. What has a serpent to do with Sacred Love?

Nonetheless my interpretation can accommodate the serpent and indeed give it the importance which it is undoubtedly intended to have. The placing of a serpent on the lap of Venus, though unusual, even unique, is not incomprehensible in this context. But to explain its meaning is to penetrate the heart of that mystery to which the Vase is both veil and entry. In accordance with our procedure so far we must first ask what does this serpent on Venus' lap in the second compartment correspond to in the first, and the answer clearly is, to the torch in the reclining Venus' hand. This torch, I suggested, was a symbol of the Evening Star. But the torch is also, I suggested, a phallic symbol, the image of a flaccid penis, an ironic comment on the inadequacy of sexual love. If this is so, then its counterpart, the serpent, is also a phallic symbol, contrasted with the torch not only insofar as it is alive and not merely burning, but also by its being made to rear upwards and not hang down. The symbol of the serpent is therefore at one with those other features of the second compartment by which it differs from the first. All of these features show Love in its more powerful manifestation, Spiritual Love, in contrast to its weaker, physical form. The Venus of the second compartment is then a Venus of the erect phallus, a monstrous idea most delicately executed. It is amusing here to recall that Wedgwood copies of the Vase in early Victorian times carefully concealed the genitals of the standing figures in the second compartment and crossed Cupid's legs. If the manufacturers had understood the female figure with the serpent to be a phallic Venus they would probably not have made their copies at all, and they would still have been mistaken since the meaning of the monstrous symbol here is that Spiritual Love is more powerful than physical love, a doctrine with which they would have agreed. As it is they mistakenly obscured some minor expressions of this same doctrine in the compartment.

This analysis of the serpent by no means exhausts its meaning. To go further we must remember that for the ancients the serpent was a symbol of regeneration, perhaps because it regularly sloughed its skin, and survived. The appearance of a serpent at the burial mound or funeral of a hero was widely regarded as a good omen for the soul of the departed, presumably because it indicated that the old dead body had been wholly cast off to reveal a brighter new one beneath. If we look closely at the serpent on the Vase we notice that it has peculiar excrescences on its head, hanging from under its throat and on the outward curve of its back. These oddities are among those which have led to its being identified as a sea serpent. But there is another possibility. Could it not be that these excrescences are the results of the serpent's being in the very process of sloughing its skin before our eyes, a process which always begins by the bursting of the old skin at the neck and then the casting of it back from the head downwards? The flaps of skin over this creature's head and hanging from the throat are the old skin of the head, and the ridge or keel on the curve of the back is the old skin already detaching from the new skin underneath. The relation of this process to that of the erect and penetrant phallus, the revealing of the hidden head, is obvious. But I would not insist upon this detail. It is unreasonable to place great stress on these excrescences. They are not by themselves sufficient basis for an interpretation, since the designer could hardly have intended just these to indicate his meaning. They may indicate that the creature is a sea serpent or that it is sloughing its skin. It may be that the creature is intended for a rather ornamental crested land serpent of a type not unknown to the ancients. The serpent form of Aesculapius at the very end of Ovid's *Metamorphoses* is a notable example.[4]

The central significance of the serpent is that it symbolizes regeneration. By placing the serpent on the lap of the Heavenly Venus the designer of the Vase indicates that regeneration is the theme of the entire design, the regeneration from Profane to Sacred Love. I have argued that the young man to the left of the second compartment is the same as the young man to the left of the first and that the design is a sequence. The robe therefore which the young man holds in the second compartment is the robe which he was wearing in the first and has just now taken off. This sloughing represents his divesting himself as far as possible of mortal concerns and the importance of this divesting, a central tenet of Platonism, is emphasized by the presence of the serpent. The serpent is on the lap of Venus because it is Venus who has brought the young man this far by the agency of Cupid and because it is only by such a divesting that the young man may know Venus herself fully. It is also possible that the designer

4. Ovid, *Metamorphoses*, 15: 622–744.

conceives of Venus as the Goddess who presides over such transformations generally. There are many such in mortal life: one is birth, when the infant puts off its mother's body to assume its own; another love, when the hymeneal membrane is broken and the prepuce pulled back; another death, when the mortal body is discarded; two others those processes to which Socrates refers in Plato's *Symposium* whereby the flesh of the body is continually replaced and so also the contents of the mind;[5] and another is the transformation represented on the Vase, from Profane to Sacred Love. It is in the context of a speech on Love that Socrates makes his points about regeneration in the *Symposium* and it is Aphrodite, I believe, who is referred to as the Goddess of painful birth and love-making in a fragment of Parmenides.[6] So it is possible that the representation of Venus with a serpent captures a conception of her role as extending right through the transitions of human existence. She may be, as it were, the Goddess at the gateway between the old and the new.

My interpretation of the Vase differs from others in two essential respects: it depends upon ratios and it identifies the majority of the figures as types, not individuals, mythological or otherwise. The thinking in ratios is characteristic of ancient thought, as much in their art, music and poetry as in their mathematics and architecture, and it is especially characteristic of the works of Plato. By making use of this habit of mind the designer of the Vase has composed two compartments which are not merely pleasantly symmetrical but in which the symmetry is the guide to their meaning. To use the letters used previously to denote the figures:

$$a/d = b/e = c/f$$

It is a commonplace that the ancient Greeks were in some sense the fathers of modern scientific thought. I agree that they were scientific and, literally, rationalist but I cannot see how their habit of thinking in ratios, of relating qualities in mutually illuminating patterns, is at all like what passes for scientific thought in our time. The Greeks were dealing with qualities, not with bare quantities.

5. Plato, *Symposium*, 207D–E.
6. Parmenides, Frag. XII.

The thinking in types rather than individuals is a characteristic of Platonism and the use of types in the composition of the Vase gives it a more universal significance than if it had represented mythological or historical scenes only. This universality is not much affected by the presence of Venus and Cupid since these are themselves universal powers. This tendency to the portraying of types may also explain the presence of the two heads dependent from the handles of the Vase. That they are dependent and not horned is clear from the continuation of the white bands on which they are suspended around the insides of the handles and from the fact that these bands are not modelled. Just as each figure in the two compartments of the Vase takes its meaning from the figures nearest to it and from its counterpart in the opposite compartment, requiring little or no mythological or historical information from outside the Vase to make its meaning clear, so also these two heads are to be understood simply by reference to their context. There is only one figure in the composition of the two compartments to which they could possibly refer and that is the figure of the thinker on the right of the second compartment, the bearded man. The two heads are the full face of this figure's profile, two tokens of the type of the philosopher. They remind us of what we may perhaps forget in considering the physical beauty of the Vase and the erotic implications of its symbols, that this design is symbolic of the power of Sacred Love, of intellectual not physical delight. But there is perhaps a conscious humour in the touching of the philosophic beard by the myrtle leaves before the opening of the arch.

It remains only to comment on the tradition, variously affirmed and contested, that this Vase comes from the tomb of Alexander Severus. The interpretation I have given of the Vase supports this tradition since the character of that Emperor, as described by Gibbon, is worthy of a Platonist. I quote Gibbon's paragraph in full:

> Alexander rose early; the first moments of the day were consecrated to private devotion, and his domestic chapel was filled with the images of those heroes, who, by improving or reforming human life, had deserved the grateful reverence of posterity. But, as he deemed the service of mankind the most acceptable

worship of the gods, the greatest part of his morning hours was employed in his council, where he discussed public affairs, and determined private causes, with a patience and discretion above his years. The dryness of business was relieved by the charms of literature: and a portion of time was always set apart for his favorite studies of poetry, history, and philosophy. The works of Virgil and Horace, the Republics of Plato and Cicero, formed his taste, enlarged his understanding, and gave him the noblest ideas of man and government. The exercises of the body succeeded to those of the mind; and Alexander, who was tall, active, and robust, surpassed most of his equals in the gymnastic arts. Refreshed by the use of the bath and a slight dinner, he resumed, with new vigor, the business of the day; and, till the hour of supper, the principal meal of the Romans, he was attended by his secretaries, with whom he read and answered the multitude of letters, memorials, and petitions, that must have been addressed to the master of the greatest part of the world. His table was served with the most frugal simplicity; and whenever he was at liberty to consult his own inclination, the company consisted of a few select friends, men of learning and virtue, amongst whom Ulpian was constantly invited. Their conversation was familiar and instructive; and the pauses were occasionally enlivened by the recital of some pleasing composition, which supplied the place of the dancers, comedians, and even gladiators, so frequently summoned to the tables of the rich and luxurious Romans. The dress of Alexander was plain and modest, his demeanor courteous and affable: at the proper hours his palace was open to all his subjects, but the voice of a crier was heard, as in the Eleusinian mysteries, pronouncing the same salutary admonition; 'Let none enter those holy walls, unless he is conscious of a pure and innocent mind.'[7]

7. E. Gibbon, *Decline and Fall of the Roman Empire*, chap. 6.

5

A CONTRARY HISTORY
OF THE WEST: 1000–2009

This is a very brief history of the last millennium in the West, from the middle ages to our own time.[1] To this period I have applied one of the standard theories of Western historiography, Plato's account of political devolution in the latter part of his *Republic*. Plato wrote that account in the light of Greek history to his own time. So we have here three histories to compare and contrast: the last thousand years in the West; Plato's account of political devolution; and early Greek history to Plato's time. In my view, Plato's theory of historical development fits the last thousand years in the West much better than it fits early Greek history. But if there really are patterns and categories which enable historical generalizations, then a theoretician may well hit on the course and sequence of a civilization entirely unknown to him.

I depart from normal practice by going backwards in time, starting at the present day and finishing in the middle ages. This has two advantages: we start from what we know; and we meet the increasingly unfamiliar in orderly stages.

Democracy

We begin exactly where we are, where Plato once was, in an advanced democracy. Democracy is the fourth of the constitutions through which the state passes in the historical process, according to Plato. This process begins with a theocracy, which becomes an

1. I am grateful to Mr. Clive Faust for much in this essay.

aristocracy, then a plutocracy, then a democracy and the state collapses under a tyranny. This is the scheme which I will apply to medieval and modern Europe. In this scheme the internal dynamic is all. The state is driven through these constitutional transformations by the struggles between its own classes.

This being so, a democracy typically defines itself by its differences from the constitutions which preceded it. These constitutions are regarded by democrats as having been founded on unjustifiable privilege. Nonetheless even under a democracy these older forms persist. So the process of democratic maturation is the slow removal of all these survivals from earlier times which block the full realization of the egalitarian ideal. In our time we call this 'the culture wars' and they were fought very passionately in Athens.

These struggles are the direct result of applying the democratic imperative to established patterns of acting and thinking. Universal enfranchisement corrodes the earlier culture which granted it, as larger and larger areas of the social life are transformed. If all are equally entitled to vote for the government, no further hierarchical distinction is possible within a society's arrangements, since there can be no power or privilege greater than this. This seems to have been true even of the democracies which Plato knew, where universal enfranchisement was still limited. As in Plato's time, so too our older democrats are often reduced to silence by this tension between their political and cultural beliefs. Strategically, the conservatives are on the defensive in this war against the progressives. The conservatives are forever having to shorten their lines as more and more territory falls to the enemy.

In our time this struggle between the earlier conservative democrat and the progressive liberationist is very clear in the shift between two ideals of education. The early democracy believed deeply in the values of a traditional education in the arts, and sought only to make this education available to everyone who could benefit from it. But latterly the content of this education has itself come into question, since it descends to us mostly from earlier phases of our history, which were tainted, the progressives believe, by their undemocratic spirit. For these reasons a new democratic theory of literature has begun to displace the works to which it applies. Faced with this and its likely consequences, the conservative may well feel moved to declare with Hector:

> *Deep in my heart, I know the time is coming when*
> *holy Troy will fall,*[2]

and he will savor, as he says it, the fear that very soon there may be no Hector with whom to say it.

In the eighth book of the *Republic*, Plato describes in detail the later phases of democratic government which immediately precede descent into tyranny.[3] He describes how, in these phases, the spirit of freedom enters even into the privacy of the home, and into the hearts of domestic animals. Parents must now yield to the wildest propensities of their children who assume all the privileges of their elders. Fathers and teachers, especially, must take great care not to appear authoritarian before their charges, and a wonderful freedom and equality obtains in the relations of men to women and women to men. The very dogs assume all the powers of their mistresses, and in the street horses and donkeys push people out of their paths with a noble disregard. Recent migrants and visitors are accorded the rights of native citizens, and those who have been condemned and sentenced for serious crimes avoid the penalties with impunity while remaining at large. There is no mention of gay liberation in Plato's catalogue, but in this respect, at least, Plato was probably as liberated as anyone.

There are other parallels between Plato's account of the later democracy and our own circumstances. In the late fifth century Plato's Athenian citizenry enjoyed considerable doles and was paid for daily service on the enormous juries of the time. For Plato this was the worst of the system, since it offended the first principle of justice, that each should be doing his own work. According to Ananda Coomaraswamy, the spirit of democratic freedom and equality grows in direct proportion to the loss of engagement in fulfilling work. It is in our own vocations that each of us is most fully developed, and where that vocation has been lost, there is a corre-

---

2. Homer, *Iliad*, vi, 447–448.
3. Plato, *Republic*, 556–566.

sponding increase in the desire for personal liberation and individual expression as surrogates.[4] This view of the relation between vocation and political freedom may have been shared by Plato who compared the processes of political devolution in the city to those in the hive, attributing a major role in democratic affairs to the drones.

Democracy is typically the business of the meddlesome, and meddling is a cardinal sin in Plato's *Republic*. Justice is doing your own work and not interfering in anyone else's. Of course, Plato's democrats were much more involved in the business of the state than today's voters. Our parliamentarians lead lives more like those of Plato's democrats. It is startling that their assembly place had room for some six thousand people only. The Athenian democracy was even more self-selective than our own. Compare the capacity of the Pnyx, where they met, with the sizes of their theatres and stadia. Democracy then and now is largely the preserve of a small minority who have the time and the inclination to manage other people's affairs. For Plato, of course, the best administrators are people who have to be compelled to do the work under threat of punishment. Who would surrender their contemplation of the Good to go to meetings otherwise?

There were two military achievements of the Athenian democracy which Plato thought wonderful. The Athenian defence of Greece against Persia at Marathon and Salamis seemed to Plato the perfection of political action. It came from an absolute equilibrium between their fear and increased obedience to law on the one side and their pride in their political liberties on the other. This is a theme we find at the beginning and end of Plato's massive oeuvre, a view which did not change. The confidence which these victories instilled in the Athenians, and their prestige among the other Greeks, were eventually to degenerate into the libertarianism of Plato's own lifetime. But those battles remained for Plato a triumph of the democratic system. A similar confidence and prestige have graced the Western democratic nations since the Second World War. But Pearl Harbour was no mass land-invasion of the Athenian

4. A.K. Coomaraswamy, *The Bugbear of Literacy* (Middlesex: Perennial Books, 1979).

homeland. From Plato's point of view, there was a certain irony in the Athenian triumph. The oarsmen who rowed the triremes at Salamis gained there the beginnings of that influence which would eventually dominate the democracy.

And Plato loved, too, the energy and variety of the world in which he matured. The paradox here is like his strictures on drama. How could an author construct dramatic dialogues in which his main speaker condemns drama? How could an author condemn the democracy in which his protagonist had the unprecedented freedom to question anyone about anything? Those discussions are the form of his art. Something similar has been said about Thucydides, the former Athenian general who wrote a history of Athens' war with Sparta. Thucydides, for all that he was once an Athenian general, supports Athens' enemies in his account of the war. But, it is said, his account of the actual events of the war is sufficiently scrupulous to enable a determination on balance, on his own account, in Athens' favour. In the same way, Plato's actions contradict his opinions.

But what could he do? A new age was upon him in which, nominally but publicly, everyone's opinion counted. The Greeks took their theories with great seriousness. This belief in each and every perspective demanded the dissolution and reconstitution of all their categories of discourse. As always happens, they were better at the dissolution than the reconstitution. Thucydides describes in detail the massive shifts in the meanings of social categories and relations under the pressure of the democratic revolutions across Greece. More profoundly still, the language of the intellect was under attack. Truth, wisdom, reality were all shifting. There was no longer anywhere to stand. So Plato, too, adopted the dialogue as his vehicle for that multivalence of opinion. In his first attempts his Socrates carefully defeated his interlocutors' claims but modestly insisted on his own complete confusion about the issue under discussion. As Plato's confidence grew, so his Socrates became more assertive but at his most strident he is still moderated by powerful objections. No philosopher, I dare say, has ever represented his opponents' views with more force than Plato in the early and middle dialogues. This, too, we owe to the democracy.

The form of Plato's dialogues is pluralist and democratic but their message is not. There is rarely a suggestion in the dialogues that all the opinions are equally worthwhile. No votes are taken. Even in the late dialogues, Socrates continues to search for some common truth despite all his disappointments. He supposes himself the possessor of infallible detectors though nothing it seems has yet got past their scrutiny. He is acutely conscious of how 'opinion is over all' in a democracy, not for want of a better understanding but as the better understanding, and he plays havoc with the logic of the proposition that everyone's opinion is equally true. Are those people right in their opinion that not everyone is right in their opinion? But almost everyone believes that some of the opinions of other people are false. So, many more people deny that everyone's opinion is true than agree with it. So if everyone's opinion is equally true, the opinion that everyone's opinion is equally true is false, for most people. This stumbling relativism is the intellectual dimension of a much smoother operation altogether, rhetoric or the arts of persuasion. In Plato's usage rhetoric has a pejorative force, it borders on what we call spin. Rhetoric is the instrument of the chancer who knows only how to bend others to his will but not where to lead them. Rhetoric gives the appearance of dialectic but is a sham, as cosmetics give the appearance of health. Late democratic Athens was a world mediated by public relations experts.

The most visible of these experts were highly-paid itinerant teachers of rhetoric who called themselves Sophists. These were the people who hammered out the progressive ideology, the philosophers of permanent democratic revolution. They made a sharp distinction between law or convention on the one hand and nature on the other. As political dispensations favour themselves in their legislation and seek their own survival through rewards and punishments, so praise and blame, right and wrong are matters of arrangement, not of God-given precept. In the *Sophist* Plato revisits the theory that everyone's opinion is true and gives it a more dangerous twist. To believe what is false, the Sophist argues, is impossible. That is to believe what is not. But what is not, as Parmenides taught, is not. There is no such thing. There is only what is and therefore there can be no false opinion. Everyone's reading of a book, a play, a situation must necessarily be. If they believe something, that something necessarily is. To believe what is not is not to believe at all. We may put this by saying that all intentional objects of thought are real insofar as they are thought.

This way of thinking is extraordinarily liberating, and it gives an entirely new impetus to the imagination. Both the ancient Athenian and our own democracies have experienced an explosion in some of the arts, at least technologically. Democratic Athens created and developed the theatre and dramatic representation: we have developed technologies for the distribution of those arts and many others. For us as for them, a people's absorption into the mediated creations of human art allows a displacement of practical sense and direct experience. People become 'lovers of sights and sounds' and much more credulous. In a dreadful image Plato represents his fellow citizens as bound to stakes, their eyes fixed on the wall of a cave where shadows play. The shadows are shadows of stone and wooden artefacts in the forms of houses, trees, animals. The prisoners know only the shadows, know nothing of the world which produces them, but they are expert analysts of the shadows and award prizes to each other for their perspicacity.

Fashions like schoolyard crazes sweep the city. People change their lifestyles at a whim, again and again. This week a man may be a drunken habitué of the brothels; next week he is a vegetarian water-drinker. He takes up philosophy, leaves it for military training, has a spell shooting his mouth off in the democratic assembly, and then joins a business company. Is he not to be admired as the most complete of human beings, the one with the most various qualities? Above all he loves public spectacles, the sensationalism and scurrility of the dramatists, and new ideas. In this last respect four hundred years made little difference to the Athenians, for then too, "they spent their time in either telling or hearing some new thing", as St. Paul says.

Plato's democracy and our own are triumphal. We feel that we have reached a new plateau in human civilization, a fuller realization of human freedom than ever before. Pericles and his consort Aspasia began the *paean* but they also emphasized the obedience to law which enabled the success. According to Thucydides, Pericles claimed that the Athenian democratic achievement would be a beacon in human history thereafter.[5] Francis Fukuyama has argued that the end of the Cold War was in effect the end of human history, that liberal democracy is the only viable political organization from this time forward.[6] His claims are less plausible than those of Pericles since Pericles' visionary claims still stand, while the liberal democracies have already to face China and Islam.

On the other hand free speech in open assembly had always been a Greek ideal, long before democracy. There is a meeting of the Greek troops early in the Iliad where the lowest among them abuses the commander-in-chief, Agamemnon, before all his fellows in the most intemperate terms.[7] Thersites was a rabble-rouser and a coward. But he has his moment and with comparative impunity. I can think of no other army in the world where this would have been possible. I doubt very much that the speech was as free as this in the Athenian democracy's armies. But we are like the Athenians in this. Despite our precursors, we believe the history-shattering dream again.

Plato's Athenians were no inventors, though their triremes and temples were second to none. They were paid for by the funds provided by Athens' allies in their anti-Persian league. Athens showed much less invention in the applied sciences than in the arts, but in the pure sciences their thinking was very like our own, and much more original with them than it is with us. They did not land men on the moon but they did claim it was a stone. This was the view of Anaxagoras, a close friend of Pericles, and he was charged with impiety for publishing it. Convicted and condemned to death, his sentence was commuted to banishment on the pleading of Pericles. Anaxagoras was also an atomist. Protagoras, for his part, insisted that man was the measure of all things and refused to speak of the Gods. Socrates describes in the Phaedo how as a young man he had been deeply attracted to the natural sciences but had given them up as illogical and self-contradictory.[8] There was a markedly material

---

5. Thucydides, II, 41.
6. Francis Fukuyama, "The End of History", August 1989, Quadrant.
7. Homer, Iliad, 212–277.
8. Plato, Phaedo, 96A.

bent to natural science in the democracy. For them as for us, democracy defines itself against the theocracy which preceded it by finding explanations for natural phenomena in purely material causation. Is this materialism a necessary or accidental feature of the democratic ethos? Could they and we have defined ourselves against the old cosmologists by other than material explanations? For Plato it was not that the material explanations were wrong. They were true, but had an entirely subsidiary role in science.

Condemned to death under the democracy and sitting in his cell, Socrates had refused to escape out of respect for his city's laws. During his last few hours before drinking the poison, he gives the disciples with him a brief intellectual autobiography. He tells how as a young man he heard of a book by Anaxagoras which explained all the workings of nature by the operations of mind, *nous*, and how he rushed out to buy the book but was disappointed. He had hoped from what he had been told that the book would demonstrate not only, say, that the earth was round, but why it was best that it be so. But in fact, as he saw it, Anaxagoras' explanations were simply mechanical. Natural science was a matter of material processes, condensation and rarefaction and so on, but nowhere was there any suggestion that this was for the best. So, says Socrates in his cell, if I were to ask Anaxagoras why I am here sitting in my cell, he would not explain it by saying that I had decided it was more just that I remain and die. No, Anaxagoras would say that the reason for my sitting here is that my knees and hips are bent. But, Socrates continues, if my legs had made the decision, I would be twenty miles from here by now and still running.

In the *Timaeus* Plato makes the same point. Timaeus gives an account of the physical components of the eye and how they cooperate to produce sight.[9] But then he says that this mechanism is only the secondary cause of sight, though most people are satisfied with mechanical explanations. The real reason for sight is so that we should see the stars. Calculating their movements generates number in our minds and from number comes philosophy, the greatest of the Gods' gifts to us. This is the primary reason for sight. Hearing

9. Plato, *Timaeus*, 45–48.

and voice likewise are given us for the proper use of music and for rational discourse. But most people are satisfied with mechanical explanations, Timaeus says. These explanations are not untrue, just inadequate. But it is also true of our time that our sciences are rigorously anti-teleological. Is this then the connection between the materialist bent of our natural science and democracy? Most people have power as voters and most people are satisfied with mechanical explanations.

Reconciling postmodern pluralism, or sophistic relativism, with the discipline of research in the physical sciences is difficult. It is a much more difficult problem for us than for the Athenians. Their physical science was speculative, where ours is scrupulously quantitative and exact. Fifty years ago C.P. Snow supposed that in Britain there were two cultures, a literary and a scientific, and that it was essential that educated people be conversant with both. But the galloping relativism of the last fifty years has made that impossible. On the one hand anything goes on principle; on the other the rigors of repeatable scientific experimentation and observation. The Arts and the Sciences have entered into a direct opposition.

But they have two things at least in common. The first is scepticism: the relativist is deeply distrustful of claims to political expertise and doubts that any such thing exists, while the natural scientist only accepts claims which can be proved again and again. For Winston Churchill democracy was a default position, bad but better than the other forms of government. In the case of the sciences, the concentration on secondary or mechanical causes is also a default position. We have grown tired it seems, of guessing at Nature's purposes. Such guesswork, we believe, is endlessly luxuriant but quite fruitless. Instead we have attended strictly to what we can really determine, the physical causation. But that is what neither Socrates nor we wanted to know. In the sophistry and the hard sciences alike we see a deliberate mediocrity, a conscious refusal to reach. Walking into a car park at night a man saw a friend bent double under a streetlight looking for something on the ground. 'What have you lost?' 'My keys.' 'Where did you lose them?' 'Over there,' the friend replied pointing into the darkness. 'Then why are you looking for them here?' 'Because I can see here.'

Plutocracy

So much for the democratic mentality then and now. But this is only half the story of democracy as Plato saw it. The other, hidden half is debt. Democracy, we may say, floats on a sea of debt. The democrats are bound to the bankers by legal bonds, and Socrates, that ancient economist, proposed that Athens' legislation should be changed to make the repayment of loans unenforceable. The bankers should take all the risk. Usury had been an ongoing problem for the Athenians since before Solon's reforms in 594 BC. At that time indebted Athenian citizens had sold themselves into slavery, and their redemption was one of Solon's first initiatives, when he was given dictatorial powers. So the problem long predates the democracy. As Plato sees it, the origin of the problem is the simultaneous emergence of two sub-classes, spendthrifts and misers. These two subclasses are symbiotic and they are both deviant. Socrates calls them the spenders and the hoarders and he uses a term for the hoarders which we can only translate as 'businessmen' or 'moneymen'. These same two groups are powerfully represented by Dante in one of the earliest rings of the *Inferno*. Here the members of each group roll huge stones along with the greatest effort. They rush round half the circle and crash into the other group coming the other way. At the shock the two groups turn on their heels and reverse their course to crash into each other again at the circle's opposite point. This is their eternity.

In the spendthrifts the appetites are out of control, in the miser the acquisitive impulse. And once these two groups emerge and engage, the social relationships of borrower to lender, lender to borrower, become a foundation of the state. They are essentially antagonistic relationships. Even in temperament lender and borrower, accumulator and wastrel, are quite incompatible. And yet their relationships come increasingly to govern the whole people. Nor are either of these subgroups true members of the classes from which they emerge. The money-lender is not a true merchant, for money itself is not a commodity. And the spendthrift, too, has deserted a vocation to pursue his pleasures.

The democratic constitution follows the plutocratic and evolves from it. How do the bankers come to lose power to the people? As Plato sees it, the triumphant moneymen come to power through their careful nurturing of extravagance in the people at large. The businessmen's profits depend on ever enlarging consumption by others. Not that these bankers spend much money themselves, since their game is making it. Making more money is their real goal and not running the state. Running the state is an excellent way of making more money, but it is not quite as good as just making more money. This is the choice that the lenders face. Democracy is the most luxurious and sumptuous constitution of all; it is even better for making money than plutocracy. This is why the plutocracy yields to the democracy. But as it does so, the plutocrats increase their power over the people by allowing them ever more expense beyond their means. In this way democracy is a kind of substitute plutocracy. By giving people the illusion of control, the bankers bind us to themselves more tightly still.

So the plutocrats are happy enough to see the end of the property qualification for voting rights. They do not want the voter to have that property; they want it. In any case, as their power increases in the plutocracy, so does their visibility and this brings danger. Plato describes how the debtors find themselves standing side by side with the creditors in the battle line on military service, and the debtors are not impressed. They find their bankers soft and few, and this puts ideas into their heads. Why should they submit to the bankers' impositions? We may perhaps compare this to the uprush of populist sentiment in Britain which removed Winston Churchill at the end of World War II. And so comes about the first democratic revolution.

Democracy is plutocracy in disguise. The progressive democrat and the banker are bound hand and foot and the history of their dance is, as we would say, their advances and retreats in the struggle between capital and labour. Plato did not share with Dante the view that lending money at interest is itself sinful. Misers for Plato are unfortunate rather than evil. They are like the spendthrifts in lacking moderation and self-control. In the later democracy, as Plato sees it, three groups are found: moneymen, democrats and the vast bulk of the people. So profitable for businessmen is the democratic system that many people quickly become exceedingly rich, and these are the honey-makers on whom the progressive drones batten. The struggle becomes increasingly intense but can only have one outcome. Eventually the democrats appoint a leader to preserve them from the deprivations of their creditors. There is an ultra-democratic revolution in which the rich are finally killed or exiled, and the new leader, beloved of the people, takes complete power. This is the second democratic revolution. Within a short time, and after the murder of a political enemy, this leader becomes the tyrant.

The moneymen play a central role in Plato's theory of history. Taking power from the aristocracy which preceded it, the plutocracy extends the franchise to those with property. Happy to draw as many of their fellow citizens into debt as possible, they vigorously support an ever enlarging class of wastrels and spendthrifts who must serve them. At a certain point the debtors rise up and seize government from their creditors, who are not much disadvantaged by this turn of events. For the moneymen are not interested in power for itself. The honours and public recognition which go with it leave them cold. The democratic system gives their acquisitiveness even more play and they fund the new world by whatever taxes, fines and subventions the drones can extract from them. According to Plato these drones are of two kinds, beggars and crooks. The difference is that the crooks have more spirit. It is from this class of crooked drones that the progressive democrats come, and from the progressive democrats comes the tyrant.

But that is in the future. Let us turn back to that crucial figure in Plato's theory, the miser. We may nominally date the beginning of our democratic era from 1776 or 1789, and we may date our plutocracy from the accession of Henry VII, the first of the Tudor monarchs in 1485. The equivalent dates in Athenian history are 511 BC for the democracy and perhaps 650 BC for the plutocracy. I am less certain about this last date because I find Plato's theory more applicable to our times than his. For it is not difficult to discern one kind of European plutocrat across the last half millennium. He adopted a religious mask, the puritan reformer. By the most extraordinary sleight of theological prestidigitation, the miser declared himself the exemplary Christian. It had always been the miser's way to spend as little as possible of what he had acquired, to put it away and add to it. This now became a virtue instead of a deadly sin, evidence not of parsimony but of temperance. Henceforward, the ever greater accumulation of capital became the very proof of God's grace. This mentality is the origin of many of the great fortunes in Europe and America in recent centuries.

Plato, of course, was spared this cant. But he found the money-men unpleasant enough even so. They are mean-minded people bent on acquisition, and social respectability is just part of their stock-in-trade. They tend, so Plato thought, to make a display of their moral rectitude, but they act well out of fear that a loss of reputation will damage business rather than because they want to act well. Their inward nature is very well represented by their business suits. Shorn of all adornment these subfusc sheaths are testimony to their seriousness, their focus and their reliability. These are people you can invest in. The Puritan simplicity of dress shouts the same message, as did the austerities of their lives. But all that had happened was that the standard forms of avarice, a deadly sin, had been given a spiritual gloss. In our time this same austerity has produced the crass architecture of our Central Business Districts, buildings as featureless as the suits.

Businessmen can be ruthless. Plato thought that they could only really be known when they had to discharge a moral duty out of sight and without recognition. In their unpublicized dealings with the widows and orphans they showed their true nature. They have become more blatant in our time. I dare say that there is nothing in English history so horrible as the first phase of the industrial revolution. Despite my dates, that was not a democratic initiative but a most avaricious application of capital. But there is an important qualification to make here: the business subgroup is part of the merchant class. This class does not have responsibility for the other classes and certainly not for the people. In their proper form the merchants, farmers and artisans are responsible for the production and distribution of many goods, but they have no other administrative responsibility in the social order. It is not their business to govern, to have an eye to the general good. But when the theocratic and aristocratic classes have been demoted, then there is no one to look to the good of the whole.

For Plato the crucial act of the plutocracy is the alienation of land. Property previously entailed from generation to generation becomes marketable, and for the first time there appear in society people without a stake, without property or a craft. These are the drones. Plato points out that these wastrels had already been reduced to their miserable status long before they finally lost everything. The new plutocratic dispensation merely legislated still further in the bankers' interest in these cases, and then for the first time beggars appeared. By the time of the Solonic reforms in Athens in 594 BC, Athenian citizens had not only lost their land but their freedom as well. Some of those whom Solon redeemed had been transported overseas so long before that they hardly remembered their Attic Greek. Meanwhile the land which they had been forced to leave bore the marker stones of the new owners. Was this what Plato was looking back to, when he described the plutocracy? Unemployment was a serious problem in Athens at the time of Solon. There were too many people for the rather infertile land, and Solon introduced a near compulsory system of craft education to turn Athens into a manufacturing city. There were severe penalties against idleness, though not so severe as under the previous dispensation where it warranted death.

But if Plato was thinking of Solon's world when he describes the moneymen, it is hard to see how the Peisistratid tyranny which followed Solon's reforms could conform either to Plato's oligarchic plutocracy or to democracy. The tyrannies which governed many of the Greek states in the sixth century BC look more like monarchies than any other constitution and they precede the democratic fifth century, they do not follow it. Furthermore, it is quite unclear how those debtors came to be in the difficulties they were. If Plato was right, they had been led into extravagant ways. But it is more likely that Attica's soil and other natural resources successively declined in quality and quantity until it could no longer support them. And I do not like the sound of those laws against idleness. Under Solon, magistrates had a duty to enquire into each citizen's occupation. I think of Blake's proverb:

Bring out weights and measures in a year of dearth.

Something similar happened in Elizabethan England. By an act of parliament a certain class of people were denominated 'sturdy vagabonds' and the penalty was a whipping and a return to the parish whence they came. But this was problematic since their parishes might well no longer exist. There had been the dissolution of the monasteries during the reign of Elizabeth's father, and even before then there had been a long usurpation of arable land for the purposes of sheep pasturage. Country people had been turned off their livelihoods in successive waves and they had gathered in the cities and towns, along with the evacuees from the monastic hospitals. They had no way of sustaining themselves except by begging and thieving and the solution was to hang them or to send them back with a whipping. This equals in ugliness those Athenians punished for an enforced loss of livelihood by the very people who took it from them. To kill a man is a crime and so is it to steal from him. But to take away his livelihood to enrich yourself is a right enshrined in legislation. And he is subject to further heavy sanctions for his loss. This is plutocracy.

I am beginning to catch the tone of Thomas More in the first book of his *Utopia*. In these pages we read at length about conditions in England at the beginning of the 16th Century. We must be very careful here because More was himself a highly accomplished Platonist who knew the *Republic* well. There is a very real danger that More's Classical learning has shaped, even determined his perception of his own time. For it certainly sounds like a repetition of the Athenian experience. As with Solon, it is hard to make out how the pauperized were responsible for their fate. Plato's spendthrift appears here no more than there. Instead peasants were being turned off their ancestral holdings to make way for sheep, whose wool commanded high prices in the Lowlands and in the Florence of the Medicis. More takes a bitter enjoyment in the joke that in England the sheep has become a man-eating animal.

This dispossession of the poor by the rich is the index of a profound shift in the understanding of the purposes of government. In the feudal order the pattern of reciprocal duties reflected the responsibility of the great to the small, the rich to the poor. Success in the feudal arrangement meant that all these responsibilities were met by a common prosperity. We are watching here the suspension of the feudal system in favour of quite different goals. Above all, the acquisition of full treasuries. The dissolution of the monasteries, too, was essentially a redistribution of wealth. The rest of More's first book of *Utopia* discusses such questions as whether thieving deserves the death penalty when the destitution which causes the thieving cannot be blamed on the destitute.

Plato supposes that there are four social classes corresponding to the four constitutions and he relates both classes and constitutions to four metals:

PHILOSOPHER KINGS AND QUEENS	THE REPUBLIC	GOLD
WARRIOR NOBLES	ARISTOCRACY	SILVER
FARMERS, ARTISANS, MERCHANTS	PLUTOCRACY	BRONZE
LABORERS	DEMOCRACY	IRON

The process of constitutional history for Plato is the devolution of political power from the philosophers to the workers through the intermediate classes. We have examined the later part of this process. But we can see already that the table is misleading. For though it appears that each class takes precedence in turn, it is not true that each constitution is a true reflection of that class. For Plato, it is not the work of the bronze or iron classes to administer the state. When in turn each of these classes appears to take precedence, that power is itself a distortion of their real natures. For it is not the bronze class but the moneymen, not the iron class but the stinging progressive drones who have actually taken charge.

The devolution of power from the priesthood to the nobility in the middle ages begins a process of gradual enfranchisement. When power passed from the hereditary nobility to any man with enough property, the franchise was widened further. When the property qualification was scrapped, this was democratic empowerment, a liberation, and the process has continued in our time with the enfranchisement of women. This is how democracies think of themselves, even limited democracies. But Plato does not agree. He sees rather the coming to power of two very destructive cliques, the moneymen and the progressive democrats. These two groups are destructive of their own classes, even more than of society generally. The moneymen, though nominally of the merchant class, dispossess the farmers and farm workers in Solonic Athens and Tudor England and they demote craft workers to machine-hands in the Industrial Revolution. The progressive democrats are interested in politics and not in maintaining the vocations of their fellow-workers, whom they will bribe to desert that work.

In any case, Plato does not believe government is for everyone. In his view Nature doles out the crafts and professions rather sparingly. Only a few in any society are born to be carpenters or musicians or doctors. The same is true of government. The cluster of skills, the kind of knowledge needed here are of a very complex kind and few are up to the task. From this point of view, widening the franchise cannot confer this remarkable skill on more and more people at will. Are we all supposed to have evolved to a new level of multi-skilling? And, of course with any craft or profession goes the absolute requirement that the practitioner be disinterested. Professionals work entirely in the interests of their clients. What they get in return is a matter quite separate from the practice of their art. But democracy works on the assumption that each of our suddenly expert voters votes in their own individual interests.

Plato is well aware of how the franchise widens over time, but he does not suppose this to be any kind of progress. In this way, despite a host of similarities, his historical theory is fundamentally different from those of Hegel and Marx who see in history the slow liberation of the human spirit through the dialectical process. For Plato the dominance of the bourgeois and then of the proletariat are the darker phases of the historical cycle, and they precede a tyranny likely enough to call itself the dictatorship of the proletariat, but very different from what Marx imagined. Nevertheless the similarities between Plato and Marx are striking. It would be very easy to believe that Marx wrote his doctoral thesis on these books of Plato's *Republic* and not on Democritus.

For Marx the capitalist industrial era was an essential stage in the full maturation of human society. An accumulation of financial resources and of human ingenuity enabled a revolution in the means of production which favoured the capitalists at first, but which would finally liberate the proletariat from labour. In this way capitalism and technology had broken the mould which hitherto constrained human social possibility. For himself, Marx seemed to imagine this new liberated order as an opportunity to engage in the sporting pursuits of the English country gentleman, with hunting, shooting and fishing each taking part of his day. Or so at least he writes in the *Grundrisse*. In the liberation from labour through a common ownership and development of the machinery, Marx saw the goal of the race.

What would Plato have made of this? He knew nothing of the productive machinery which makes the Marxian utopia at least conceivable. But like Solon, Plato would have deeply disapproved of being liberated from work. The first reason that Plato gives for the division of labour is not that it meets society's needs best if each of us does one thing to the common benefit. The division of labour answers exactly to our own innate predispositions. Dividing labour enables each of us to do the thing we are best fitted to do and this is the source of happiness. Justice is doing your own work and no one else's. But in Marx's Manifesto state capital is to be used to expand mechanical industry and so remove the crafts which were after all only a temporary phase, in Marx's view, for all their sentimental associations. I imagine that in Marx's state everyone would still be following the crafts and professions as hobbies, and putting out the products of their labour for collection by the rubbish cart. Let the labourers run to fat or pay to waste their powers on the treadmill of a gym. From Plato's perspective, as from the early Christian, the accumulation of capital brings trouble, both to the miser and to the state.

Here is a Platonic history of mercantilism in our time. First the moneymen began to dispossess the farmers by enclosing their tillage and forcing them off the land. Now the earnings of the farmers flowed into the pockets of the moneymen. The urban proletariat so created was treated with great brutality. This process went on for centuries. Three centuries later, machinery was developed which reemployed the labouring class but dispossessed the craft-workers who were forced down into the proletariat. This change, too, was fully legislated for and enacted with great brutality. Now the wages of the craft-workers flowed into the pockets of the moneymen. Work with the new machinery was mindless and could be performed more cheaply by children than adults in many cases. Around 1800 England's economy depended on the labours of 400,000 children under the age of 14, few of whom reached the age of 30. Nearly two centuries later new technology enabled the displacement even of factory labour, whose wages now flowed into the pockets of the moneymen. Larger and larger proportions of the population came to live on handouts and antidepressants. But there is a real sense in which liberation from factory labour is a liberation, so this stage of the decline is, I suppose, a relative progress. In Plato's view a very large part of any population is disposed to farming, the crafts and general labour, and these people are losing one of the most important human rights of all, the right to live out their lives doing their own work. Where new technology has not displaced our factory labour, cheaper labour overseas has, and so the ruinous process spreads over larger and larger areas of the earth. How many nations now have been put through their own industrial revolutions?

Aristocracy

Our historical retrogression brings us to the end of the middle ages, to the 15th century. We now leave a world more or less controlled by liquid capital for a quite different order. Why did feudalism yield to mercantilism? Because the aristocratic government, for all its high ideals, was too interested in money. This is Plato's explanation. We can put this together with Plato's explanation for the yielding of the plutocracy to democracy, that the moneymen are too intent on making money. In respect of historical causation, Plato agrees with St Paul that the love of money is the root of all evil. The historian R. H. Tawney supposed that the feudal order collapsed as a result of its own success. So wealthy had Europe become that the wealth broke the confines of the social order which produced it, and reconfigured the constitution. This is an abiding problem of social organization: how to remove the surplus without damage to the system. For all the fulminations of Jehovah at the fall of Adam, it is still easy to maintain oneself in nature. I have heard said that Aborigines needed to work only eight hours a week to sustain themselves. This makes that proud boast, the Australian eight-hour working day, look very arduous.

The later middle ages employed two standard techniques for disbursing the surplus, massive building programs at home and military adventures overseas. The surplus was literally sacrificed, made over to spiritual purposes, at least nominally. The entire resources of the age, the wealth, the skills and the intellect were realized in the cathedrals, and they remain the clearest possible evidence of those peoples' success even from this time so far beyond them. It was material success since they remain among the greatest buildings we have, but it was also a spiritual achievement since those resources were devoted to worship. The crusades were much less splendid, an effervescence of animal spirits. Dying for Christ makes much less sense in full armor on a foreign battlefield than it ever did naked before the lions in the Colosseum. But there were close connections between the building of the cathedrals and the crusades. From the consecration of the abbey church of St Denis in 1145 the Gothic order of architecture had transformed cathedral style. The Gothic by its use of light and precious materials manifested the splendor of God and St Denis was also the home of the *Oriflamme*, the standard of France. Compared to the austerity of the Romanesque, the Gothic style evinced courtly ideals in much the same way as the crusades.

Gothic cathedrals are vast and comprehensive. During the performance of their rites they bring together in a single place and time all their theoretical and practical sciences in a single staggering integration. Those people were much more adept than we are at holding all their experiences and understanding before their minds simultaneously. Perhaps it was this discipline which enabled them to see God's plenty all around them, for this is the sense which their art gives us. It was not a material plenty in the first place but a spiritual one, a plenty so enormous that the sheer number always threatens but never quite overwhelms their capacity to comprehend it. How many souls do we meet by name in Dante's other worlds? Let them stand for the dead who are constantly with us. Consider now the worlds to whom Chaucer introduces us in the *Canterbury Tales*. Blake thought Chaucer's twenty-nine pilgrims an exhaustive account of the major human types. What makes all this possible of course, is systematization. The better organized our categories, the more detail we can accommodate. The later middle ages owed much of their intellectual reach to their monkish predecessors, who were forever on their feet during theological moots shouting '*Distinguo*'. By means of these distinctions the nine orders of angels could be adequately and exactly defined in relation to each other, while the deeds that earned the saints their places in Paradise were compendiously recorded in the Golden Legend.

Though thinly populated, Europe during the later middle ages had a crowded mental life. Like their imaginative world their social word was systematic:

> *God bless the squire and his relations*
> *And keep us in our proper stations.*

And there were a great many stations and precise degrees of social standing. From our point of view this systemization was restrictive because it did not reward merit, but birth, and Plato would have entirely agreed with us. But there is another criticism to make of the social systematization, and that is that it was simply excessive in itself, whatever its social consequences. Late medieval social organization suffers from a hypertrophy of the administrative function. Thomas More when Lord Chancellor remarked that it would take an Englishman his entire life to learn the laws by which he was supposed to live and this was in the early 16th century. The same affliction had struck liturgical practice as we learn vividly from Erasmus's *Praise of Folly*. Europe was succumbing to a kind of legalism. As much may be said of the massive *Summae Theologiae*, which seem to us to want to fix too much. Too much of the letter, too little of the spirit.

As for privilege of birth, Plato supposed that the best breeders under the best circumstances produced the best issue. But he did not believe that this was scientifically determinable even at the highest level. So people are going to be born in classes to which they do not belong. The health of the state depends on putting people in the class they merit, not to which they are born. So for Plato the class system of the later middle ages is unsatisfactory, as is any aristocracy of birth. Exactly the same may be said of the Hindu caste system which was a meritocracy according to the Laws of Manu. The administrative detail in an aristocracy masks this fundamental deviation from the proper order. Even at this early stage of the European story, when we are still in Christendom, the constitution has departed from the model.

The nobleman's privilege of birth came at a price. The first part of that price was that he was never anyone who could take pleasure in his spectacular, unearned advantage. From his birth almost he was constrained by duties which multiplied as he matured to the point where he was entirely encircled and animated by the elaborate roles he had inherited. To fail in their performance was utterly to betray himself, so that his very life or death became just a commodity in the scales of honour. A warrior noble was doubly bound, first to the family of whose honour he was the living guardian and symbol, and then to his lord. His ideal was death fighting justly on the field of battle. Not so much a person as a personification of a code. And so the flags and the fanfares and that other compendious study of the middle ages, heraldry. There is something Homeric about bloodlines and the assurance with which those people could compute up, down and between their family trees as a matter of universal significance.

The aristocrat of this era is the diametrical opposite of the progressive democrat. Of that figure Coomaraswamy supposed that his loss of any real vocation had been replaced by a desire for personal liberation and individual expression. But it is quite unclear what that freedom and individuality are. Ruskin speaks of their 'vain, incoherent, destructive struggling for a freedom of which they cannot explain the nature to themselves.' As for the notion of the individual, it is in modern times correlative to the notion of the mass. An individual is someone distinguished from the mass, which of itself is very little distinction indeed. The notions of the mass and the individual are, of course, products of the industrial revolution which obliterated the old craft categories and depressed craft-workers into the proletariat. In modern societies the construction of the 'individual' personality seems largely a matter of whimsy, a selection of marques. We may give more sense to the notion of the individual when we think of those stridently non-conformist puritans, except they were all so exactly alike. But the kings and nobles of the late middle ages were hardly individuals at all. We think of them typically in the act of self-dedication to an altar, a lord, a quest. And we may compare that sense of family to the *lares* and *penates* of the old Roman nobility and the chapels where stood the busts of their ancestors.

According to Ruskin, people who know how to live are people who have found something which they would rather die than compromise. So the pastor will die rather than deny his faith; the soldier will die for his country; the merchant will die rather than break his bond; the master craftsman will die rather than betray the standards of the work. Clearly these people do not think of themselves as individuals primarily but as members of classes. Maintaining their membership is more important to them than personal survival. These people have more than their mere numerical identity, they have achieved quality.

We may contrast the freedom of the democratic individual with this peculiar freedom of the dedicated worker. Individual freedom is like the freedom of the open road, choosing ones course of action from an indefinitely large range of possibilities. And we can imagine people who quite literally commit themselves to this freedom and become entirely free molecules, vagrants with no links to anyone or anything. Against this we may set the freedom which comes from the mastery of a discipline or science. Consider a violinist in a symphony orchestra. Here years of training finally enable a vigorous cooperation with others of the same kind, a full expression of the violinist's feeling for the music from that place in the orchestra. Here the freedom comes from the subjection of the trainee and from the rigorous observing of exact limits within the ensemble. These are the terms in which the Prayer Book speaks of our relation to God, whose service is perfect freedom. Now it may be that the freedom to choose to be a violinist is necessary to becoming free as a violinist, but even this is not entirely clear. On the other hand the freedom to choose is vacuous if it does not lead to a worthy model or ideal. These models and ideals were much clearer in the middle ages than they are now, and they were carefully organized in relation to each other. At the centre of that organization were the Royalty and Nobility.

The centrality of the aristocracy is most easily represented by the Platonic theory of the three souls of which each human being is composed. They are the intellect, the passions and the appetites. This crude tri-partition does not distinguish between lust and gluttony, for example, or between anger and brotherly love, but it does allow a dynamic model of the person and the state. Intellect should control appetite by means of passion. The philosophers should control the lower classes by means of the warrior-auxiliaries. When we are drawn to some base action by our appetites, we should control ourselves by becoming indignant. We should reprimand ourselves sharply and express disgust that we could even think to stoop to such a betrayal of ourselves. In Plato's example a man catches sight of the Athenian executioners depositing the bodies of their victims outside the city walls. The man wants to look at those corpses but knows that he should not. In this inner struggle the appetite is matched by an emotional attachment to a sense of his own self-worth.[10] Inwards, as a means of self discipline, is the proper direction of anger. Similarly *jihad* is the inner war against oneself before it is an outer struggle. Plato is said to have asked a friend to beat a slave for him, since he was angry and so could not do it himself. Here is a struggle between the inner and outer wars, between passions.

That sense of ones own self-worth is rather more than the sense of ones human rights. Plato's insight is that much of the human emotional apparatus is there to assist the intellect in its direction of the whole being. If we think of the heart as the seat of the emotions, the belly of the appetites and the head of the intellect, then the passionate heart guards the pass between the appetites and the intel-

10. Plato, *Republic*, 439–440.

lect. The heart does two things: it reflects the wisdom of the intellect in the forms of noble ideals and models; and it is sufficiently dominant to control the appetites. There are things we care about more than our own physical satisfactions. When our appetites impede our gaining of those nobler goals we are justly angry with ourselves, and this strong feeling is how intellect exerts its sway.

The nobles similarly exercise authority over the commons. But Plato explains at length how they must have a double character, gentle to their own but fierce against external enemies. The training of the nobles to this double role Plato compares to the training of watchdogs who must learn to discriminate between friend and foe and act appropriately. The dog is a useful emblem of the aristocracy for a further reason: it is remarkable for its loyalty. Plato also supposes this class to be somewhat adolescent, in comparison to the philosopher priesthood. This is a further development of his psychological theory. The spirited or passionate element in the personality responds rather to images and pictures of truth, justice and love than to the principles in their pure form. Typically this class is less intelligent than the philosophers and cannot discern the principles and the Good from which they depend by means of the dialectic. But they have excellent natures and are very moved by actual instances of these ideals. Their training therefore must introduce them to stories about noble deeds and admirable people whom they will naturally seek to emulate. So given are they to hero worship that the models they encounter will always influence them. So the greatest care must be taken in the choice of those models by the philosophers.

A strong feeling for the right when properly trained will serve as an excellent guide to the moral life. It has been deeply inculcated but it is not itself understanding. It is right opinion, not knowledge. If you have been to Megara, you know the road to Megara and nobody can mislead you. But if you only know of the road to Megara, however accurate your knowledge, you can be persuaded to try another path. In the same way, however passionate the commitment of the aristocrat to the ideal, he is not entirely proof against seduction from his proper course, and this is what happens when at last the aristocracy yields its pre-eminence to money and the plutocracy. At that time they lose the inward struggle against the appetites and not only because those appetites have grown. Rather, uncertainty and disaffection have already divided the citadel of the heart.

In the middle ages the ideals of courtly love exemplify the victory in this inner *jihad*. It is an instance of Platonic love. The lady is idealized, the devotions are never ending, consummation denied. The sword between the lovers in the bed. What matters here is the indefinite prolongation of those more subtle ideals and sensations in the first moments of an affair. The passion is held suspended between the purely spiritual adoration of the Godhead and physical union. According to Plato the upshot of such a passion, if entirely uncontaminated by so much as a kiss, is a major step towards Heaven by the two lovers at their deaths.

Courtly love raised physical love to the level of the passions and held it there. The Gothic style of cathedral architecture may be said to have had the opposite effect on the spirit. Compared to the Romanesque style of architecture which preceded it, the Gothic was flamboyant and gorgeous. The Gothic reduced the spirit to the passional level as it had raised physical love to that same level. From 1145 when Abbot Suger consecrated the church of Saint Denis, the old austerity yielded to Gothic extravagance. And so this is the date from which I suppose the aristocracy to have achieved pre-eminence over the priesthood. The church of Saint Denis was the home of the *Oriflamme*, the banner of France, and was thus the religious centre of France's national spirit. Abbot Suger himself also served as Regent of France, at the apex of the country's secular administration.

Suger wrote a book to justify his revolution in architecture and church decoration at Saint Denis. There was a clear case to be made against his program. In the epistle to the Hebrews, the apostle argued that all the paraphernalia of Jewish worship had been superseded by the sacrifice of Christ. Where Moses had prescribed a yearly sprinkling of the sacred objects of tabernacle and temple, the blood shed by Christ at the crucifixion purified the people and their places of worship once for all. Saint Bernard, the great Cistercian and a contemporary of Suger, made use of comparatively humble altar vessels in his order, but Suger's chalice, carved from a single onyx, and mounted with gold and gems, is one of the wonders of the jewellers' art. Suger justified such splendor by arguing that all the most beautiful things in nature should be exploited for that supreme human act, the celebration of the mass. And even then, he wrote, they would fall far short of the splendor of Christ's sacrifice. But theologians had also argued that it impeded true worship to imagine the glories of the spirit and of the angels in the form of golden figures arrayed in light. The Gothic order introduced almost all the forms of wealth into the practice of Christian worship. In this way the pre-eminence of the aristocracy marked itself off from the priestly simplicity which preceded it and from the primitive austerities of the reformers who followed.

We may think of the differences between the Romanesque and the Gothic, between the monastic priesthood and the aristocracy, as complementary rather than antagonistic. The priesthood represents the inwardness of God, *Deus absconditus*; the aristocracy represents the glory of God. In the same way Plato's idea of the Good is absolutely invisible and to be known at only the very deepest level of the mind, while the child of the Good, the sun, faithfully reproduces outwardly in the world of sight the entire structure of the intellect. So does the aristocracy represent the divine at the physical level. At the same time, the show of the aristocracy is a mirror of its own power, and it is chastening to realize how many of the forms of art that we love for their beauty were also assertions of dominance. The modalities of power were much more subtle in those days.

The Romanesque is stable, dim and contemplative. The Gothic is aspirational. In the aristocratic phase, the quest is greater than the goal. The delicacy of the Gothic poise is itself a risk. Titus Burckhardt compares the Renaissance to the state of the soul which has deserted the faith. The psychic energies which devotional practice had balanced and developed were suddenly released in a welter of new artistic possibilities whose very splendor blinds us to how far they deviate from any spiritual normality. This is too harsh a criticism of the Gothic, but it is certainly true that in its striving there is some loss of the spiritual centre. At great cost Suger represented at Saint Denis, in altar and periphery, the throne of God and the angels. But, after all, church and choir and altar are finally merely the outward expressions of God's only real temple, our hearts.

Theocracy

Once there were fine, resplendent times when Europe was a Christian land, when one Christendom occupied this humanly constituted continent. One great common interest united the remotest provinces of this broad spiritual realm. Without great worldly possessions, one Head guided and unified the great political forces. A numerous guild, to which everyone had access, stood directly beneath him and carried out his behests and strove with zeal to confirm his beneficent power. Every member of this organization was universally honored, and if the common people sought comfort or help, protection or counsel from this member, and in return were happy to provide generously for his manifold needs, he also found protection, respect, and a hearing among the more powerful, and everyone cared for these chosen men, equipped with miraculous powers, as for children of Heaven whose presence and favor spread manifold blessing abroad. Childlike faith bound men to their pronouncements. How cheerfully every man could fulfill his earthly labors when, through the agency of these holy persons, a secure future was prepared for him and every misstep forgiven, when every discolored spot in life was obliterated by them and made clean. They were the experienced helmsmen upon the great unknown sea, in whose keeping one might disdain all storms and count on a sure attainment of the coast and a landing at the world of the true home.[11]

So wrote the German Romantic Novalis. Novalis was no Papist but his praise is unstinting. We must now consider how far the Church met the Platonic account of the philosopher rulers. Certainly the priesthood escaped Plato's strictures against belonging to a class by right of birth rather than by merit. The priesthood was a clear meritocracy to which admittance was gained by intelligence and devotion. Insofar as the priesthood was celibate there could be

---

11. Novalis, *Hymns to The Night and Other Selected Writings*, "Christendom or Europe", tr. Charles E. Passant (USA: The Liberal Arts Press, 1960), p. 45.

no question of succession. Were Plato's philosopher rulers celibate? No, but their relations to their spouses were most peculiar. Both men and women were philosopher rulers in Plato's *Republic* and Plato supposed that humans should propagate with great care, for the best eugenic results. For this reason marriages were to be arranged strictly for breeding purposes, though the public announcement was that all these unions had been specified in detail by the Delphic Oracle. No child knew who his parents were in the higher classes but called all those older parents or grandparents, all those the same age brothers or sisters, all those younger sons or daughters. In these ways Plato hoped to have the benefits of the breeding program without the disadvantages of nepotism.

Why did the theocracy yield to aristocracy? According to Plato's theory, the philosopher kings and queens eventually began to make mistakes in their application of the astronomical movements of the sun to the purposes of human conception. Also they began to favour their own children over others by a corruption of the communitarian system of generational but not family relations. Here we have a clear difference between the Platonic and medieval histories. I know of nothing to suggest that the rise to power of the nobility was the result of a failure in an astronomical application by the Church. And even if it had been, there is no way that the astronomical application could have affected the energies of the priesthood, for the purpose of producing their successors from themselves, since they were eunuchs for Christ, in theory if not in fact. Even if they produced children, these children had no rights in the Church, nor ever came to have. The *Republic*, on the other hand, required elaborate defenses against nepotism. But it is true that there were families of popes, like the Colonnas and Medici, and in this way the early papacy was corrupted.

The Church denied itself both the advantages of breeding from its best specimens and the engagement of women at its higher levels. On the other hand Abbot Suger who inaugurated the Gothic order and was regent of France came from peasant stock. That is meritocratic. We may certainly compare the educational ladder in the *Republic* with the rigors of taking orders, but there was nothing in the priests' education to compare with the intense mathematical speculations demanded of the philosopher ruler. Boethius had helped transform the Platonic curriculum into the seven liberal or inferior arts, of which the last four correspond to Plato's mathematical disciplines. But the emphasis is quite different: there is no sense in the curriculum that the manipulation of mathematical numbers and figures prepares the soul for its conversion to the vision of the Good.

If the Church did not produce speculative mathematicians, it did produce metaphysicians, ontologists and epistemologists. The goal of the Platonic search is contemplation of the real, which is eternal and divine. But Platonic contemplation is more than matched by the inwardness of the Church. The beatific vision might be another version of the Platonic vision of the Good, but for the fact that contemplation itself had clearly developed since Plato's time. In particular we find one mode of contemplation in the Church which has few parallels in Classical antiquity, the apophatic or negative path. This path leads to the goal by the systematic denial of all attributes whatsoever to God, including divinity.

Even so, Plato's philosopher rulers have much less contact with the other classes than the Christian priesthood does. To rule is a burden for philosophers who want only to contemplate, and so they may have to be driven by the threat of punishment to do their duty by the state. All forms of work are essentially a service done for others which is why people are paid for them in the other classes. But the philosophers rule in the interest of others to repay the state for having trained them well. Though they work for others, their work does not seem to require that they mix with them. In the early Church extensive provision was made for both men and women who wished to withdraw from the world in contemplation. But, as Novalis describes, priests were very active in the world as the immediate spiritual guides of people at every level. Plato's philosopher rulers had seen the vision of the Good and knew the end of life, but they could hardly communicate this to those ignorant of mathematics. The priests, on the other hand, were expert in the comfort and care of even the weakest among their many charges.

One area of the common life which was of the greatest concern to the philosopher rulers was the organization and coordination of the crafts and professions. Justice is doing your own work and not interfering in anyone else's. It is the duty of the administration to ensure this. Justice is the critical moral category in Plato, the one which determines ones life after this one. In the theocracy at last we arrive at a constitution in which all the classes are in their proper places. It is true that nobody should enter the Academy who was ignorant of geometry, so that the highest vision in Plato's system was reserved for scientific contemplatives. In the Christian order there was no such restriction. But it is also true that each of the crafts and professions was contemplative in the Platonic under-standing. The craftworker must contemplate the idea of the artefact to be made; the farmer the idea of the creature to be grown; the pro-fessional the idea of health or justice or truth. The alignment of these ideals with vocational practice was the philosopher rulers' concern.

We hear little in Plato about that other dimension of ancient craft practice, its assimilation to the worship of the Olympians. It is a strange task Plato undertakes. He provides the most complete account of the operations of the spirit and he does so without refer-ence to the deities of his people. But they are always in the back-ground and they stood, in part, for the crafts and professions. This aspect of work was realized again in the middle ages by saintly patronage. Sacred to particular saints, each of the crafts enjoyed a holiday on its saint's day, so that all the forms of work were taken up into the spiritual life of the people. There are still remnants of this, especially in central Europe. Stories of how patron saints had helped workers in their vocation reinforced the notion that work was a spiritual path and a form of sacrifice leading to self-realiza-tion. And clearly in this early period the Church played the domi-nant part in the determination of the forms of the fine arts and their appropriate subjects. Exactly in the same way the philosopher rulers censored music and turned away the dramatic poet from their gates.

In the early Middle Ages the moneymen did not exist. Usury was a deadly sin because money does not reproduce itself according to nature. The moneyman turns his face against both God and nature when he resorts to this method of making a living. It has been said that these rules were partly for the protection of the poor against the power that unscrupulous lenders could acquire over them. In the *Republic* Socrates accepts the view that even the buying and selling which shop keepers do is not fully human work, but is reserved in well-governed states to those who are weakest in body and useless for any other task. In this way those who are more capable are free to pursue their crafts or farming or haulage without having to waste time waiting for customers in the marketplace.

How affluent were the bronze and iron classes in the *Republic*? Temperance is their guiding virtue, though they are at least permitted contact with money, unlike the gold and silver classes. Under the medieval theocracy the earnings of an artisan covered the maintenance of himself, his family, the tools of his trade and an apprentice. The last item here is characteristic of the forethought taken to secure the continuation of the work. It is reminiscent of the concern shown at the beginning of the Hippocratic Oath both to protect and to propagate medical science. These requirements precede the better known injunctions on how doctors should conduct themselves professionally with patients.

By our standards a medieval artisan working on the terms outlined would be living 'at subsistence level' and we would be moved to rescue him and his family from their impoverishment. But there is reason to believe that a skilled artisan living at subsistence level is much better off than a modern factory-hand with his own motorcar. We may recall here Coomaraswamy's dictum that when traditional workers meet, they talk about their work; when modern workers meet, they talk about the ballgame. Coomaraswamy even suggests that our real motive in seeking to help these people is that we begrudge them their calm and contentment. We are all progressives now and anyone who does not strive to better themselves beyond their present lot has forfeited their right to be considered a participant in the human enterprise. They are country bumpkins fit only for the dustbin of history. This is where we have put our own ancestors from the earlier middle ages, though we can hardly condemn them for being an evolutionary dead end. We think of that time now as the dark ages, without realizing that its obscurity may spring directly from our own lack of vision.

The dark ages are growing darker. What we have from the period before the end of the first millennium is not susceptible to our historical methods: lives of the saints; Church history; knightly tales. In all three there is an element of the supernatural, of miracles and fairies. For Tennyson in the *Idylls of the King* or for Keats in *The Eve of St Agnes*, these stories enlivened the imagination and enabled the recreation of those times. But the Enlightenment had already moved on from such sentiment and demanded hard data. So the only entry we have into the period is narrowing generation by generation, except for the countervailing force of archaeological finds. One solution to the dilemma was suggested by William Blake, that the people of those distant times simply had more senses or more enlarged senses than we do, and actually did see spirits everywhere. According to a 17th century Anglican bishop, Richard Corbet, the fairies left England from the time of Queen Elizabeth, first for Wales and the west country and then across to Ireland.

> But since of late, Elizabeth,
> And, later, James came in,
> They never danced on any heath
> As when the time hath been.[12]

What corresponded to the Christian theocracy in the earliest Greek history? Where did Plato get his *Republic* from? By his own account his Socrates may have been guilty of an unconscious plagiarism in his setting out of the ideal state. We are told in the *Timaeus* that Solon heard from the priests in Egypt that nine thousand years before, Athens was just such a state and had such a constitution as Socrates described. Unfortunately this is on an altogether different time scale from the one we have been using. Is there anything nearer in time to the first millennium B.C. which could have served for Plato's model? It is hard to see how Homer's world could have done so. And yet again was this not very like Saxon England where the marvellous churches, illuminated manuscripts and jewelry, seem to have coexisted side by side with the internecine warfare of gangs of

12. Richard Corbet, *The Fairies' Farewell*.

aristocrats? The *Iliad* opens with the humiliation of the king of kings by a priest of Apollo. Chryses' daughter, Chryseis, had been captured and awarded to Agamemnon as spoil; her father wanted her back; Agamemnon refused abusively; the priest prayed to Apollo; Apollo sent a plague on the Greeks; Agamemnon is forced to submit; he returns the girl with a sacrifice of a hundred oxen to Apollo. One man, on his own, overpowers the entire Greek army and its commander-in-chief, and this is the opening of Homeric epic. Theocracy or what? Still, I defy anyone to read Plato's *Republic* into the *Iliad* or *Odyssey*. It is much easier to read the *Republic* into the priestly world of the early middle ages.

What is the source of theocracy and what does it supplant? In the case of Christendom, one engaging answer to this question was given by the German Romantic, Heinrich Heine: the late Roman empire exhausted every last sensation of tongue, touch, eye, ear, sex organ and, no doubt, the soles of the feet. Where was there to go? Only out into the desert, hair shirts, thorns and flagellation as the last resort of a flesh almost inured to sensation. Within emergent Christendom the explanation of its triumph was the agency of the Holy Ghost and the sacrifice of martyrs. For Plato the origins of theocracy are more complex. He supposes periodic holocausts and cataclysms of which the only survivors remain in the mountains long ages after the disaster. Tentatively they reclaim the plains from the wild animals, and a new round of the historical cycle begins. In a myth Plato tells a more fantastic story. The solar system, he says, is beautifully organized by God and in perfect order when he sets it going and it goes by itself. But slowly over aeons like all things bodily, it begins to wobble and a degree of disorder sets in. Classes of things which were previously distinct begin to merge and produce strange hybrids and the cosmos tips into 'an infinite sea of dissimilarity' where the various kinds lose their proper characters. Once there were strawberries, ice and cream, but then... When this disorder reaches a certain point, God steps in and takes hold of the cosmos and *winds it back in the opposite direction.*

Everything goes into reverse. People are born into the world out of the ground and they are old and white-haired, but they grow younger until at last they grow tinier and tinier and disappear. This reverse cycle continues for many revolutions until at last all is accomplished in that direction and God releases the cosmos once more. At that moment those people who had been born white-haired and old, and had with time grown into their early adulthood, suddenly found themselves growing old again and returned eventually to the earth. The ultimate reason for this double cycle is quite simple. The cosmos could not be allowed to remain forever in the same act because this is the prerogative of its maker alone. Of all changes reverse motion in the same place is the simplest. So the cosmos *must* go both ways. And you will appreciate, dear reader, that in anticipation of that happier reverse cycle, we too have just reviewed Western history backwards.

Here again, as with Solon and the Egyptian priests, we are dealing with entirely the wrong timescale for our purpose, which was to locate the theocracy at some point within Plato's historical range. With the priests it was a mere nine thousand years. With the cycles under consideration here, between holocausts and cataclysms on the one hand and the reversals of time itself on the other, we are even more out of our depth. But these Platonic theories do provide explanations of how some historical cycles begin, and not simply by cultural revolutions. And the double cycle of time provides a context for Plato's view of history in our part of the cycle as a decline from a better age when God has just let the newly reorganized cosmos go its own way. This surely is where Plato's ideal state itself belongs, near the beginning.

This essay would have been much more difficult to write and publish at almost any other time than now. If it were not for the postmodernism of the last generation, it would have been much harder to see how our world mirrors the sophistic relativism in Plato's ultra-democratic Athens. If, again, we had already slid into the tyranny which Plato supposed to follow democracy, then the essay might have been written but would have had to go unpublished except by *samizdat*. As it is, we seem to have all the parts of Plato's analysis to hand in our own history and present. And this completeness suggests another speculation, that we have here all the principles and elements necessary to an exhaustive historical and political sociology. At any given time the four classes are in some configuration or other in their relations to each other. These relations may be represented by a simple table of sixteen squares arranged as a square:

	PRIESTS	NOBLES	TRADERS	LABOR
PRIESTS				
NOBLES				
TRADERS				
LABOR				

Each square in the table corresponds to the view taken by one or another class either of itself or of another class. The square on the extreme left of the top row is the priesthood's view of itself. Next to it in the top row is the priesthood's view of the nobility. The square on the extreme right of the bottom row is labor's view of itself. We now reproduce this table of sixteen square three more times, so that we have four such tables, one for each of the four constitutions. These four tables set out the views of each class of itself and of the other classes through the course of the historical declension from theocracy through democracy. Of course, the four class system is very crude and in any case the classes themselves begin to sink into 'the infinite sea of dissimilarity' as the historical process develops. Nonetheless our system of sixty four class perspectives does have the advantage of looking systematic and exhaustive. And we must remember that the process is cumulative, by reaction and absorption, so that earlier class perspectives are carried up into the later ones in many different ways.

The fourfold table has another application. Plato was a man formed by a democracy but one who rejected it. This is why he is so infuriating at the present time. He is no relativist though he understands deeply how each historical period creates laws and constitution in the interests of its own dominant class. Each constitution does it, except for the theocracy which governs in the interests of all. And this is where Plato ceases to be a relativist. His model of history is a perfect social order followed by successive deviations in an identifiable pattern leading to final collapse. So the four copies of the table are not co-equal: the theocratic table is the template of the other three. In that table the relations between and within the classes are optimal, while in the other tables those same relations are more or less deformed. All this is strikingly similar to his account of the animal kingdom: human beings are the template and all other creatures are deviations from this norm, down to snakes and then fish.

The idea of a template with deviations appears both in his narrative of constitutional devolution and in his devolutionary zoology. As he describes the series of constitutions, each new deviation is represented politically in the class struggle, but also personally in little pictures of the choices faced by someone or other deciding how best to live. In this way the historical development becomes an immediate moral degeneration through a long series of private misjudgements. But if we accept that Plato supposed that some things were very right and others very wrong, then this way of pointing up moral questions is much more adult and pertinent than the usual morality tale. As the various constitutions unfold we learn exactly what not to do. Do not lend or borrow; avoid democratic assemblies; avoid idleness; do the work to which you are fitted and do not interfere in anyone else's. But the moral focus has completely changed. Our living as we should no longer depends on our meeting contemporary norms, since in many cases those norms are precisely the deviations against which we are being warned. Plato's morality is always unconventional in every age but the first. The great lesson seems to be that we should find as traditional a craft or profession as we may and practise it as a service to others.

Platonists do not march in the vanguard of history. They discern the same direction in history as the progressives up to the point of tyranny, but they regard it as a decline of which tyranny is the culmination. But Platonists are not political reactionaries either, because they take no part in politics. They are what the democratic Athenians called 'idiots', very private citizens. There have been no Platonist revolutionaries, though by an accident of birth or circumstance there have been some fine Platonist rulers, even of the Roman empire. Platonists have made up their minds that the current of history is against them. In the later stages of the cycle, not only history but the current of popular opinion will also be against them, since Platonists do not share in the joys and enthusiasms of capitalism or democracy. To the Platonist, progress as we have it now is 'a kind of ecstasy for mugs', and most of the technology is merely the way the rich take the wages of work from the rest of us. Platonists are born old. From their early teens and even earlier they remember with a passion a time when things had not decayed.

For no one at all is happiness a matter of keeping step with history. History is like fortune, very fickle. Find the work for which you are best equipped and do it. You will be an anachronism, and most of all in this, that you are as fully in use and of use as you can be.

6

HATRED OF NATURE

The application of modern technologies on a vast scale has damaged the natural environment in certain ways. It is often argued by North American and British theorists of the environmental movement that Westerners cause and tolerate this damage because they are Christians. For in the view of these theorists Christians believe that God gave people the world to do as they would with it. Moses wrote in *Genesis* that God gave mankind 'dominion' over the whole of creation. This Biblical view, the theorists argue, has underlain and justified that destruction of the natural world which the West has perpetrated since the late Eighteenth century.

The writings of Francis Bacon in the early Seventeenth century furnish a brilliant instance of this nexus between the Bible and our new technologies. Bacon supposed that the complete enslavement of Nature to human purposes by the systematic application of the experimental method would bring about the return of humankind into Paradise. This was an Eden transformed, indeed, by our full scientific control of all that it contained, but which answered as perfectly to our requirements.[1]

But was Baconian science a Christian science? The fact that it was a new kind of science was the greatest claim to fame of Bacon and his followers. They were going, they believed, where no one had gone before. The Christian sciences which developed in the fifteen centuries to Bacon's time knew nothing of his visions. The Mosaic teachings concerning our place in Nature had left the European environment comparatively undisturbed for a millennium and a

1. I am grateful to Mary Midgley, *Science as Salvation: A Modern Myth and its Meaning*, 1996, Oxon, Routledge, for much of this essay.

half while its inhabitants looked to salvation from above. The natural world had been safe under the protection of the Universal Church. The problem followed the Schism.

But the Bible may still be to blame because Bacon could read it as justifying the enslavement of Nature. This is a much milder attack on Christianity than the one with which we began and it does not remove the difficulty. We may put the matter quite scientifically: the moral force exerted by the Universal Church in respect of Nature over fifteen centuries of European development acted uniformly in one direction. Then the European attitude to Nature began to change. As any physicist knows, such a phenomenon is only explicable on the assumption that another force has come into play. And this new force cannot be Christian teaching or tradition because that is the old force.

What was the new force? It was consequent upon the Schism and gave a different account of Nature from the teaching of the Universal Church. Though Bacon dressed his vision in the rags of *Genesis*, his Paradise was essentially, not just accidentally, a secularization, a turning away from the spiritual understanding of Nature which had prevailed in the West up to his time. Bacon's promises of scientific salvation had more in common with Satan's offer to Jesus of dominion over the kingdoms of this world, and with Satan's offer to Eve when he gave her the apple. We should be very careful to scrutinize the small print when we make a deal with the Devil. Otherwise we might find that we do indeed gain the world which the Devil promised, but in so corrupted a state that it is not worth having.

To suggest that Bacon was Satan may seem a touch extreme, but this was exactly how William Blake regarded Bacon at the turn of the Nineteenth century. Blake bracketed Bacon with Locke and Newton in a Satanic triumvirate which held the European mind in subjection. About Newton Blake was wrong though he could not have known it. Works of Newton, never published even in part until the 1960s, reveal that Newton understood gravity as the same spiritual force which governed the musical intervals. Newton argued that the ancient Greeks had known this. Locke was a prosy amateur who never once referred to Plato's works in his endless rejection of innate ideas. But Bacon was something else. For him Nature was to be harried, pierced, penetrated, tormented, and shaken to her foundations. As Attorney General, Bacon racked an aged clergyman to extort a confession to treason and has been universally condemned for it.

Bacon was a favorite and courtier of King James I who had super-intended the mass torture of witches and published a book on the subject. The King's research was certainly one prototype of Bacon's experimental method, and Bacon's account of his method is shot through with the language of violence against women. Quite as vicious and even more unctuous in King James' service was William Shakespeare, who composed for the King's Players the unspeakable *Macbeth*. This was the most misogynistic work of art to appear in the West before the books of de Sade. As king, James lived in fear of being murdered by witchcraft. He believed that witches were regi-cidal because kings were the regents of God on earth. Macbeth's murder of good King Duncan, James' counterpart, at the urging of Lady Macbeth and the three witches realized James' fear and must have strengthened him in his own murderous persecutions of women. Shakespeare's play enacts an apocalypse in which the hid-den womb of Nature turns against creation and destroys its own offspring in embryo. Lady Macbeth declares to her husband that she would rather rip a smiling infant from her breast and dash its brains out than break such an oath as he has sworn to murder Dun-can. Early in the play the witches allude to their harassment of a ship at sea. This echoed James' own experience at sea when he brought his bride from Denmark. They were nearly wrecked by a storm which James believed to have been raised by witches. For James, Shakespeare made Satan manifest in certain women and finally in Hecate herself.

Shakespeare stoked James' fires but Bacon found the more horri-ble solution in the long term. With the complete enslavement of Nature and all her children, Bacon anticipated the truly masculine birthing of time, *vere masculum partum temporis*. The twist here is the tension between the middle two words. Parturition is the defining act of the female as begetting is of the male, but Bacon looks forward to the dawn of a new age when parturition too will be the prerogative of the male. How better protect the world from the inverted destructiveness of women than by taking the power of giving birth itself from them? This is the exact reverse of the Virgin's giving birth in the Gospel. We can see dimly in Bacon here, with hindsight, the cloning and test tube babies of our own time. For my part, at this point the image of James in the torture chamber metamorphoses into all the vivisectionists. It was necessary to shake Nature to her foundations, to test her to destruction, in the methodical pursuit of her innermost secrets.

Blaming Christianity for the destruction of the natural world occasioned by anti-traditional modernity is neither plausible nor reasonable. It is more plausible to blame Christianity for the condition of women in our time. But it is no more reasonable. Bacon's modernity aimed precisely at the displacement of women from their most sacred and mysterious powers. Finally these people want to steal motherhood itself, as Huxley imagined in *Brave New World*, where a whole population is conceived, gestated and born, or rather decanted, in mechanical farms. For the denaturing of the environment and of womanhood in our time we need look no further back than Bacon's inklings of 'the scientific age'. I applaud the Catholic church, though I am not a Christian, for its defence of women against this greatest evil.

7

GRAVITY AS HARMONY

In certain unfinished notes which have only recently been published, Isaac Newton asserted that one of his laws of gravity was known to Pythagoras twenty-two centuries before him. Newton claimed that one of the laws which made him famous had been known in a quite different way at the very beginning of our era. He explained how he came to this view:

> For Pythagoras, as Macrobius avows, stretched the intestines of sheep or the sinews of oxen by attaching various weights, and from this learned the ratios of the celestial harmony. Therefore, by means of such experiments he ascertained that the weights by which all tones on equal strings [were produced] were reciprocally as the squares of the lengths of the string by which the musical instrument emits the same tones. But the proportions discovered by these experiments, on the evidence of Macrobius, he applied to the heavens and consequently by comparing those weights with the weights of the Planets and the lengths of the strings with the distances of the Planets he understood by means of the harmony of the heavens that the weights of the Planets towards the Sun were reciprocally as the squares of their distances from the Sun.[1]

Pythagoras hung weights from strings tied to nails and by altering the weights and the lengths of the strings discovered the relations between the weights, the lengths of the strings and the tones. This experiment revealed that a tone is produced in the next highest

1. McGuire, J.E., and Rattansi, P. M., "Newton and the 'Pipes of Pan'", *Notes and Records of the Royal Society* 21, 1966, p.p 108–143.

octave by a weight four times as great as a given weight on the same string. But the same note in the higher octave is also produced by the given weight on a string half the length. So the same note is produced by halving the string or quadrupling the weight or by any combination of these two methods within this range. Similarly the twelfth is produced with a third of the string or nine times the weight.

Now if we compare the tensional weight on the string to the force of gravity and the length of the string to distance in space, it is the same law or ratio which governs the relation between the weights and the lengths of the strings and which governs the relation between the force of gravity and distance in space. In its balance between the length of its strings and their tensions, the lyre or harp is a little model of the relationship between gravity and distance in the solar system. This was the insight which Newton attributed to Pythagoras and his followers in the *Classical Scholia* to propositions 4 to 9 of Book II of the *Principia Mathematica*.

In the published versions of the *Principia*, Newton had been quietly insistent that his laws were not hypothetical. In his statements of them he had, he wrote, carefully avoided going beyond the evidence of the phenomena of the tides and planets from which he had inferred them. He had, he admitted, nothing to offer as to the cause of gravity. He had merely established the formulae which described its effects. Newton's contemporaries in Europe were less than satisfied with this thesis which eschewed any physical or metaphysical speculation. On the other hand there can be no doubt that much of the work's appeal lay in its requiring no leap of faith, no cosmological assumptions. But if many of Newton's readers were content with this, he himself was not. He wanted to know the cause of gravity, not merely how it worked. His laws as stated did not satisfy the inward querist in Newton himself and his notes show him at his extended search. These two different approaches to his own laws correspond to two different kinds of science: the experimental, empirical and positivist approach of the *Principia* against the traditional approach of the *Classical Scholia*.

The published *Principia* was the very type of the experimental philosophy and it is ironic that the greatest exponent of this method

was not satisfied by it. That Newton researched alchemy and biblical prophecy and chronology is well known. It is less well known
that just where he had made his greatest breakthrough he continued
to search for understanding of a more traditional kind. The unpublished notes show his conviction that he had had some success in
this search. The fact that the same ratio governed the relation
between the tensions and lengths of strings as governed the relation
between gravity and distance suggested to Newton that what we call
gravity the ancients had called harmony. But to call it harmony rad-
ically alters our perception of this force. The new name demonstrated the connection between the objective laws of nature and the
subjective sensations and experiences of, say, a musical audience.
The same rightness may be felt in the dispositions of the planets as
in the intervals of the scale. But in that event, as Newton saw, the
inner worlds of sensation and pleasure are aligned with the outer
world of physics. So the source of gravity or harmony may be a
thinking being who has organized the world in a way which may
reasonably be regarded as intelligent. Gravity ceased to be a blind
force and instead became evidence in its own nature of a divine
intelligence in the framing of the world. Here is Newton again from
the *Classical Scholia*:

> And since all matter duly formed is attended with signs of life
> and all things are framed with perfect art and wisdom and
> nature does nothing in vain, if there be an universal life and all
> space be the sensorium of a thinking being who by immediate
> presence perceives all things in it, as that which thinks in us,
> perceives their pictures in the brain: those laws of motion aris-
> ing from life or will may be of universal extent. To some such
> laws the ancient philosophers seem to have alluded when they
> called God Harmony and signified his actuating matter har-
> monically by the God Pan's playing upon a pipe and attribut-
> ing music to the spheres made the distances and motions of
> the heavenly bodies to be harmonical and represented the
> Planets by the seven strings of Apollo's Harp.[2]

2. McGuire and Rattansi, op. cit., pp 108–143.

For Newton, as for his contemporaries, there was no necessary division at all between the scientific and the religious. On the contrary, as for the Greeks, scientific enquiry led to a more profound spiritual understanding. On this evidence Sir Isaac Newton was not the first of a new order of scientists who deposed the metaphysical speculations of his predecessors. He was, rather, one of the greatest of all traditional cosmologists. But the *Classical Scholia* were not published until the 1960s. I wonder if the publication of the *Classical Scholia* closer to Newton's own time might have made a difference to the division between science and faith which seems so problematic now. The European authority of Newton, established by the *Principia*, might have swayed the balance.

The understanding of the spiritual order revealed by science and mathematics is not a matter of understanding the latest physics. On the contrary, the simplest forms of the numerical and geometrical systems elicited from the Pythagoreans their most devout response. In the number four, the square number, the triangle, they could see the forms of a spiritual life. They did not need to know about protons, neutrons and electrons. To the same end we might examine the elementary astronomy and geography of Homer and Parmenides. These two are the first scientists of our era whose work has come down to us in any quantity. With Pythagoras they were taken by the Greeks to have established the sciences of astronomy and geography, and what they did for the Greeks they do for us also since our sciences descend from the Greek. The verses of Homer and Parmenides were interpreted in ancient times to describe the terrestrial and celestial spheres: their poles, equators, tropics and polar circles. The descriptions are precise but they are simultaneously descriptions of mythological and ritual events.[3] Why should we not believe, as the Greeks did, that the human understanding of nature through science is one of the most profound spiritual paths open to us?

The intellectual history of the West over the last three centuries is the story of how a religion without a natural science has slowly

---

3. R. Sworder, *Science and Religion in Ancient Greece* (San Rafael, CA: Sophia Perennis Books, 2008).

yielded to a natural science without a religion. It may be that the Western church, in one or other or all of its forms, generated the new science which was so unlike itself, and that for this reason science developed as it did in the West and nowhere else. But it is quite clear that the origin of the Western scientific tradition was ancient Greece and that a large part of this tradition's established results are ancient Greek discoveries. From this point of view the Christian centuries appear, rather, as a long interlude in a greater drama which connects the latest phases of our era more closely to the very first, the ancient Greek, than to any other since. For all that, our science now is not Greek science. Plato supposed the natural, moral and mathematical sciences to be a ladder to mystical transcendence, through a meditation on the faculties of cognition. If the sciences were so for us, then the Academy would return to the worship of its founding deities, the Muses and shining Apollo.

8

KEATS AND PSYCHE

Ode to Psyche

O Goddess! Hear these tuneless numbers, wrung
    By sweet enforcement and remembrance dear,
And pardon that thy secrets should be sung
    Even into thine own soft-conched ear:
Surely I dreamt to-day, or did I see
    The winged Pysche with awakened eyes?
I wander'd in a forest thoughtlessly,
    And, on the sudden, fainting with surprise,
Saw two fair creatures, couched side by side
    In deepest grass, beneath the whisp'ring roof
Of leaves and trembled blossoms, where there ran
    A brooklet, scarce espied:

'Mid hush'd, cool-rooted flowers, fragrant-eyed,
    Blue, silver-white, and budded Tyrian,
They lay calm-breathing, on the bedded grass;
    Their arms embraced, and their pinions too;
    Their lips touch'd not, but had not bade adieu,
As if disjoined by soft-handed slumber,
And ready still past kisses to outnumber
    At tender eye-dawn of aurorean love:
    The winged boy I knew;
But who wast thou, O happy, happy dove,
    His Psyche true!

O latest born and loveliest vision far
    Of all Olympus' faded hierarchy!
Fairer than Phoebe's sapphire-regioned star,

Or Vesper, amorous glow-worm of the sky;
Fairer than these, though temple thou hast none,
         Nor altar heaped with flowers;
Nor virgin-choir to make delicious moan
         Upon the midnight hours;
No voice, no lute, no pipe, no incense sweet
     From chain-swung censer teeming:
No shrine, no grove, no oracle, no heat
     Of pale-mouth'd prophet dreaming.

O brightest! Though too late for antique vows,
     Too, too late for the fond believing lyre,
When holy were the haunted forest boughs,
     Holy the air, the water, and the fire;
Yet even in these days so far retired
     From happy pieties, thy lucent fans,
     Fluttering among the faint Olympians,
I see, and sing, by my own eyes inspired.
So let me be thy choir, and make a moan
         Upon the midnight hours;
Thy voice, thy lute, thy pipe, thy incense sweet
     From swinged censer teeming;
Thy shrine, thy grove, thy oracle, thy heat
     Of pale-mouth'd prophet dreaming.

Yes, I will be thy priest and build a fane
     In some untrodden region of my mind,
Where branched thoughts, new grown with pleasant pain,
     Instead of pines shall murmur in the wind:
Far, far around shall those dark-clustered trees
     Fledge the wild-ridged mountains steep by steep;
And there by zephyrs, streams, and birds, and bees,
     The moss-lain Dryads shall be lulled to sleep;
And in the midst of this wide quietness
A rosy sanctuary will I dress
With the wreathed trellis of a working brain,
     With buds, and bells, and stars without a name,
With all the gardener Fancy e'er could feign,

Who breeding flowers, will never breed the same.
And there shall be for thee all soft delight
That shadowy thought can win,
A bright torch, and a casement ope at night,
To let the warm Love in!

We do not know how much Keats knew of the work from which the subject of his poem is taken. The story of Cupid and Psyche is part of the *Metamorphoses* or *The Golden Ass* of Apuleius, from which it is often excerpted. We do not know whether Keats had read the work as a whole. We do know that for the story of Cupid and Psyche he used the translation of the Elizabethan Sir William Adlington, a contemporary of George Chapman, Keats' favorite translator of Homer. Keats did not need to use the Adlington translation since there was at least one other available to him written much more closely to his own time. This was by an author with whom he was acquainted, Thomas Taylor the English Platonist. There is evidence that Keats was more or less personally acquainted with Taylor. In his letters there are two references to Taylor, and it is possible that Keats makes use of Taylor's introduction to the fable of Cupid and Psyche in his poem.[1]

What does Keats mean by the fane or temple which he mentions in the first line of the last stanza? It is generally agreed that this temple, and indeed the whole of the landscape in which it is set, are metaphors for poetry. In order to worship the goddess Psyche, Keats will not build an actual temple but a temple of words. The temple, the trees which surround it, and the landscape in which all is set are metaphors for the act and product of the creative imagination. He writes

Where branched thoughts, new grown with pleasant pain,
Instead of pines shall murmur in the wind.

The trees which surround this temple, 'dear as the temple's self', are thoughts and the 'pleasant pain' with which they are grown is

---

1. Letter to Benjamin Bailey, May 28, 1818. Letter to George and Georgiana Keats, February, 14, 1819.

the comfort and discomfort of the creative process.[2] Later on in the stanza he talks of 'the wreathed trellis of a working brain', and in this conceit of the trellis he has found an analogy to poetic structure. The structure, like the trellis, is a support for the ideas of the poem, on which those ideas are woven. Like the structure of metre and rhyme, the trellis is regular and composed of parallels. The notion of a poetic temple is by no means confined to this poem, although we cannot say how far Keats was aware of his precursors. It is to be found in the works of Pindar and Virgil.[3]

Where then is the poem which Keats promises to write in the last stanza of the *Ode to Psyche*? There is nothing in what he wrote after composing the *Ode to Psyche* which could possibly qualify. There are a number of possible explanations for this. Perhaps, though he intended to write the poem, he was unable to do so because of his early death. Perhaps it was a poem that he never intended to write down, a poem of the mind, for his own purposes, which he had no intention of making public. It was to be composed in some untrodden region of his mind, and it was to stay there. It was to be a poem of the 'working brain', a composition to which he could always return.

Certainly this final stanza is a poem of the mind in a quite different sense. It is a celebration of consciousness, in which the poet finds metaphors for a special alertness and serenity in his own state of mind. In the lines

> *Far, far around shall those dark-cluster'd trees*
> *Fledge the wild-ridged mountains steep by steep*

the panoramic vision which the poet provides as a metaphor for his state of mind gives the reader a sense of having been lifted up above the world like a Yogi in some mountain fastness. The distances which are viewed from this vantage bespeak the clarity of the medium through which they are observed. But it is not only a visual clarity.

---

2. *Endymion* 1:28.
3. Pindar, e.g., *Olympian* i, 6: *Pythian* vi, 5 ff: Virgil, *Georgics* iii, 8–22.

And in the midst of this wide quietness

gives us a sense of how consciousness pervades the entire region, listening to the silence. This is a mind at peace with itself, rejoicing in its own limpidity, in its awareness of all directions.

There is another possible explanation for our failure to find a poem of this description in the works which Keats composed after the *Ode to Psyche*. It may be that the poetic temple which he describes in the final stanza is that stanza itself. A poetic temple is no more than the description of a temple, and this stanza is itself just such a description. Where else than in the stanza are we to find the things which Keats describes, since their whole existence is merely in their being described? The obvious counter-argument against this supposition is the series of future tenses which occur throughout the stanza. The temple which Keats is describing is something that he *will* build. This series leads us to expect something beyond the poem, but in this we may be misled. Indeed, one use of the future in such contexts has been given a grammatical name, the *performative future*. In a most unusual way the poem which the poem describes can be said to be making itself in the very process of our reading it. The verbs of the stanza usually appear at the beginning of the sentences in which they occur. By the time those sentences are concluded, what the future verb has promised at the beginning of the sentence has been performed. The simple experiment of replacing the future verbs with present ones reveals something else about their use in this stanza. They give it a driving force, an onward rush, an intensity of commitment, which the present tense can in no way convey.

Then there is the immediacy with which Keats evokes the landscape of the mind which he describes. The repetition of 'far' at the beginning of the fifth line requires that the voice of the reader deepens or rises in order to express the vastness of the view which these words describe. By this modulation the vastness of the landscape is brought before the mind's eye of the hearer. The same must occur with 'in the midst of this wide quietness'. From the line before, the reader's voice is hushed, and in that hush we feel the silence. Where else are we to find this world which Keats describes than in the very act of his describing it? This gives a special meaning to the lines

> *With the wreathed trellis of a working brain,*
> *With buds, and bells, and stars without a name,*
> *With all the gardener Fancy e'er could feign,*
> *Who breeding flowers, will never breed the same.*

It is as though these lines conjure the things which they name into existence; the various ornaments of the trellis are brought into being before our eyes. We stand here at the moment of creation, at the edge of that deep Romantic chasm from which the world emerges.[4] The self consciousness of the last stanza is foreshadowed in the first, where the poet uses the expression 'soft-conched' of Psyche's ear. Even within the context of the line in which it appears, it is unlikely that this word 'soft-conched' is merely an elaborate expression to describe the whorls of his goddess' ear. He is asking pardon of the goddess for singing her own secrets to her, and the mention of a shell in relation to an ear in this context reminds us irresistibly of the old fancy that one can hear the sea in a sea-shell, though far inland. Of course, what is heard is not the sea but merely the echoing silence of the ear which hears, and this is a happy image of the way in which the goddess is about to hear her own secrets sung back to her. The proximity of this relationship between shell and ear, between the goddess and her own secrets, points forward to the intense self awareness which characterizes the final stanza. Just as the ear hears itself in the shell, so in the final stanza the poet describes the very act of his composing of his description.

On this interpretation of the final stanza, Keats is doing something which is not without parallel in the history of English poetry. We may call poems which describe the act of their own composition, works of literary self reference, or perhaps, following Kant, transcendental poems. One well known example of this is *The Coronet* by Andrew Marvell. In this poem Marvell describes how he is wreathing a garland of flowers with which to crown his Saviour. As he weaves it he finds within it a serpent which he cannot remove without breaking the wreath which he has made. He concludes not

4. S. T. Coleridge, *Kubla Khan*, 12.

with the crown, but with the flowers of this broken wreath around the feet of Christ. In this poem the flowers and the wreath are all of them images of the poem itself. But in this case the self reference is accidental. It is a literary device of considerable charm, but it is not, we feel, essential that he treats his worship of the Saviour in this way.

This is quite different from the literary self reference of Keats' poem since Keats is writing a poem about his own soul. It cannot be accidental that he should compose the last stanza of this poem in this self conscious way. The self reference of this stanza, as I have interpreted it, must in some way reflect his understanding of his soul. Throughout this last stanza he moves ever closer to grasping the very principle of his own awareness, and it is this principle, we may take it, which he supposes to be represented by Psyche. But this is to make Psyche stand for rather more than has been supposed previously, even by critics who appreciate the self reference of the final stanza. She does not 'analogize the perfectly fulfilled, unlimited, visionary imagination', but the immediacy of consciousness itself.[5]

Keats, Apuleius, and Cupid

Let us now consider the relationship between Keats' poem and Apuleius' fable. One respect in which they differ is in their treatment of Cupid. Cupid appears twice in Keats' poem, in the first two stanzas and in the very last line of the last. In the first stanzas he is seen lying with Psyche on the grass; the two are at once people, butterflies and doves. But it is when we think of them as butterflies that the first stanzas work best. The lines describing the flowers are like a photographic close up, and the embrace of their pinions recalls the way in which butterflies fold into each other in their mating. Of these two the poet, as he wanders thoughtlessly through the forest, recognizes one immediately, 'the winged boy'. Why, we may ask, does he recognize Cupid more readily than Psyche? A winged boy need not be Cupid, it might be Hermes. I suggest that the recognition of Cupid

5. M.L. D'Avanzo, *Keats' Metaphors for the Poetic Imagination* (Durham, NC: Duke University Press, 1967), note 20, p. 213.

by the poet is immediate because Cupid is the poet. There would be some superfluity in the poem if there were two admirers of Psyche, and the poem would then leave open the question of the relationship between them. Keats could certainly describe himself as a winged boy. He was young and by no means tall, and his wings could be the wings of the poet, 'the viewless wings of poesy'.[6]

In the final stanza Keats declares how he will build a temple. This temple is comparable to the palace to which Psyche is brought. In the very last lines Keats describes the poem not as a temple, a trellis, nor a sanctuary but as 'a bright torch' and an open window 'to let the warm Love in'. These are sexual symbols of the male and female, but they are much more than this. If we take it that the final stanza is a case of literary self-reference, and that this self-reference is essential to Keats' understanding of the relationship between Cupid and Psyche, then the torch and the window represent the function of the poem in a quite special way. By means of these images Keats is explaining how the poem itself is a means to the reintegration of himself with his soul. Psyche is accessible to him through the poem; the poem enables him to recover that self-consciousness from which it derives. On this account the poem is primarily an aid to meditation. This is what is meant by letting the warm Love in. In this case, Keats, as poet, as self, must be the Love who is let in. The sexual union represented by torch and window is an image of the still more profound and wonderful union of the self and the soul.

It is this spiritual union which the lovers in the first stanzas have temporarily foregone, separated as if by a slumber which is also described by Wordsworth.

> Our birth is but a sleep and a forgetting[7]

and by Blake

> When the soul slept in the beams of light.[8]

In both Apuleius' fable and Keats' poem there is the river or

---

6. *Ode to a Nightingale*, 33.
7. W. Wordsworth, *Ode: Intimations of Immortality*, 58.
8. W. Blake, *Auguries of Innocence*, 128.

brooklet in the forest which surrounds Cupid's palace. This brooklet is the stream of Forgetfulness, Lethe, which prevents us from full awareness of our own true nature. Keats describes it in *Endymion* as

> *the fragile bar*
> *That keeps us from our homes ethereal.*[9]

The bar is fragile for the same reason that the brooklet is 'scarce espied'. The veil of ignorance which keeps us from the knowledge of our own souls is, from the point of view of that knowledge, quite unreal. Again, those who drink of the waters of Lethe, waters which no vessel can hold, forget first of all that they have drunk.[10] So for both the regenerate and the unregenerate the waters of Lethe are very hard to espy.

But if the poet thinks of himself as Cupid, then he has exactly reversed the relationship between Cupid and Psyche which we find in the fable of Apuleius. There quite clearly Cupid is the divine principle to which Psyche aspires. Through her reunion with Cupid she is made immortal herself. Cupid is the immortal, Psyche the mortal for the greater part of the story. In the Keats' poem however, the situation is exactly reversed. Psyche is the goddess from the very beginning, to whom the poet expresses his devotion. It is the divinity of the goddess which so inspires him. This is why he deprecates himself in the opening lines.

In Keats' poem Cupid is the poet. Who is Cupid in Apuleius' fable? In his Introduction to his translation of the fable, Thomas Taylor claims that Cupid is pure Desire.[11] Presumably he is Desire because he is Love, and he is pure because he is not to be seen but should remain invisible to Psyche. When Psyche looks upon him, the purity of the desire is lost as far as she is concerned and hence he departs. To think of Cupid in this story as Desire is in my view unsatisfactory. What does it mean to say that Psyche is in love with

---

9. *Endymion* I, 360–361.

10. Plato, *Republic*, 621A.

11. T. Taylor, *A Dissertation on the Eleusinian and Bacchic Mysteries*, in *Thomas Taylor the Platonist*, eds., K. Raine & G.M. Mills (Princeton, NJ: Princeton University Press, 1969) pp. 382 ff.

Desire? In a famous aphorism La Rochefoucauld said that a woman falls in love for the first time with her lover, and ever afterwards she falls in love with love itself.[12] This certainly gives some sense to the proposition that Psyche falls in love with Desire, but it does not seem to fit the story at all. Cupid is a divinity through association with whom Psyche herself becomes an immortal. He is also the master and perhaps the builder of the palace to which Psyche is blown at the beginning of the fable. Cupid is not the personification of the feeling of desire. He is rather, I suggest, the creative power called Eros by the Orphics, who was regarded as one of the very first and most powerful of all the gods. This is the god of whom Parmenides speaks in the thirteenth fragment of his poem.

Eros, the very first of all the gods, (she) devised.[13]

This same god appears very early in the *Theogony* of Hesiod, and in a paraphrase from Pherecydes it is explained how Zeus has to become Eros in order to make the world.[14] If this is the Cupid with whom Apuleius' Psyche falls in love then their relationship is symbolic of the soul's aspiration to the supreme creative principle. That principle is invisible and to be known only through introspection, but it is also manifested in the world which both reveals and conceals it. Hence when Psyche looks upon this Cupid with her eyes, she at once learns more of him and loses him.

For Apuleius the Platonist, the god Cupid may be a way or representing what Plato calls 'the Demiurge', the supreme creative principle. For the poet Keats, Cupid is a representation of the mortal poet as he pursues the principle of consciousness. No difference, we feel, could be greater than that between these two views of Cupid. Yet when we compare the overall pictures offered us by the two authors, the differences do not seem very great at all. The fact that Keats reverses the roles of Cupid and Psyche in his account of the story does not much alter the meaning of that story as it appears in

12. Le Duc de la Rochefoucauld, *Maxim 21.*
13. Parmenides, Frag. XIII. For the subject of the fragment see Plutarch, *Dialogue of Love,* 756E.
14. Hesiod, *Theogony,* 120: Pherecydes, Frag. III.

Apuleius. Certainly the method of enquiry, introspection, is the same for both poet and Platonist. The path consists in turning one's back on the external world, the back wall of the cave, and proceeding to a discovery of the inward nature of the soul which projects those images previously taken for real. So Keats asks himself in the first stanza whether he has seen the winged Psyche with awakened eyes or has merely dreamt it. Form the point of view of the unliberated consciousness, the vision of Psyche is nothing but a dream. From the point of view of the realized consciousness, the vision of Psyche is the reality and the external world is the dream. When Keats asks himself whether he has seen Psyche with awakened eyes, he is not asking whether he has seen Psyche out there in the world. He is asking whether at that time he had awakened from the dream of mortal life to a knowledge of the really real, to use Plato's phrase. For Plato and Apuleius and Keats, true knowledge is knowledge of the higher self and it is gained by introspection into the nature of consciousness.

Temple and Palace

Let us now compare Keats' temple with Apuleius' description of Cupid's palace. To begin with Adlington's Apuleius:

> [Psyche] fortuned to espy a pleasant wood invironed with great and mighty trees. She espied likewise a running river as cleare as crystal: in the midst of the wood well nigh at the fall of the river was a princely Edifice wrought and builded not by the art or hand of man, but by the mighty power of God: and you would judge at the first entry therin that it were some pleasant and worthy mansion for the powers of heaven. For the embowings above were of Citron and Ivory, propped and undermined with pillars of gold, the walls covered and seeled with silver, divers sorts of beasts were graven and carved, that seemed to encounter with such as entered in. All things were so curiously and finely wrought, that it seemed either to be the worke of some Demy god, or God himselfe. The pavement was all of pretious stones, divided and cut one from another, whereon was

carved divers kindes of pictures, in such sort that blessed and thrice blessed were they which might goe upon such a pavement. Every part and angle of the house was so well adorned that by reason of the pretious stones and inestimable treasure there, it glittered and shone in such sort, that the chambers, porches and doores gave light as it had beene the Sunne. Neither otherwise did the other treasure of the house disagree unto so great a majesty, that verily it seemed in every point an heavenly Palace, fabricate and built for Jupiter himselfe.[15]

According to Thomas Taylor we should interpret Apuleius' account of Cupid's palace in the following way,

When Psyche is represented as descending from the summit of a lofty mountain into a beautiful valley, this signifies the descent of the soul from the intelligible world into a mundane condition of being, but yet without abandoning the Heavens. Hence the palace which Psyche beholds in the valley is, with great propriety, said to be a 'royal house which was not raised by human, but by divine, hands and art.' The gems, too, on which Psyche is said to have trod in every part of this palace, are evidently symbolical of the stars. Of this mundane, yet celestial, condition of being, the incorporeal voices which attend upon Psyche are likewise symbolical: for outward discourse is the last image of intellectual energy, according to which the soul alone operates in the intelligible world. As voices, therefore, they signify an establishment subordinate to that which is intelligible, but so far as denudated of body, they also signify a condition of being superior to a terrene allotment.[16]

According to Taylor, then, Cupid's palace is some way between the intelligible and physical worlds, a halfway house in the soul's descent from heaven into matter. This makes sense but I am not

15. Apuleius, *The Golden Asse*, trans. William Adlington, 1923, London Nonsuch Press.

16. Taylor, op. cit., pp 430–431.

completely convinced by it. The palace was divinely built and seems to have been built for gods. The precious stones which comprise the pavement may be symbolical of the visible stars, but they may also be symbolical of stars as purely intelligible beings according to the astronomy which Plato describes in the seventh book of the *Republic*.[17] The walls are sealed with silver on which are engraved many kind of beasts. It is easy to suppose that these pictures of beasts are in fact the ideas of the creatures in nature. But in this case, for the purposes of this story, it is more plausible to suppose that Cupid's palace is symbolical of the intelligible realm itself and not of some state between the intelligible and the physical. It is true that Psyche is seduced from this palace by the machinations of her sisters when she is persuaded to look upon Cupid with her eyes although he has expressly forbidden it. If, it may be said, the palace represents the intelligible realm, how can we explain Psyche's fall? Why is she not completely satisfied with this supreme condition? But according to Platonists there is indeed a fall from the intelligible realm, however hard that may be to understand. It is notable that Psyche at one point says to her husband:

> Sweet husband I had rather die than to bee separated from you, for whosoever you bee, I love and retaine you within my heart as if you were myne owne spirit.[18]

If that is the feeling of Psyche in the palace, then she is completely united with Cupid, although she does not know that he is Cupid. The palace is itself the heart of which she speaks. It is in this heart, the seed or core of the universe, that all the things in physical nature are to be found in principle.

From another point of view, we may feel that Keats's description of Cupid's palace is somewhat overheated. This is in sharp contrast to the opening lines of Keats' description of his temple. Here is no pleasant wood but a wild secluded scene 'in some untrodden region' of the mind. The trees are the astringent pine, their branches 'grown with pleasant pain', mounting 'steep by steep' the wild and precipi-

17. Plato, *Republic*, 530A.
18. Apuleius, op. cit., v. 6.

tous mountain sides. There is a sense of space and vistas, quite different from Psyche's feeling of imprisonment in Cupid's palace according to Apuleius' story. To be sure, this sense of wild nature, somewhat unusual in Keats' work, is soon tempered by his description of the softer elements in the landscape. For once Keats has avoided the temptation of entering into the luscious too early, and both this stanza and the poem as a whole benefit. On the other hand Keats has considerably softened the effect of the beasts engraved upon the walls which seem to encounter Psyche as she enters the palace. Instead Keats gives us two catalogues;

> *And there by zephyrs, stream, and birds, and bees*
> *The moss-lain Dryads...*

and again

> *With buds, and bells, and stars without a name.*

These two lists suggest the plenitude of the landscape, which corresponds to the plenitude of the pictures engraved in Cupid's palace. In both cases it is the diversity or variety of the creatures which is striking. This is similar to Plato's account in the *Timaeus*. In that dialogue the creative powers are described as wishing to create the fullest possible variety of creatures in order that the creation might be as complete and therefore as perfect as possible. According to Professor Blackstone, Keats was influenced by the *Timaeus*, especially in the composition of *Endymion*.[19]

Notable also is the way in which Keats' creatures are for the most part either numinous or fanciful: numinous because they are nature spirits like zephyrs or dryads, or fanciful like the flowers on the trellis. In these respects they are like the creatures of Apuleius' palace as interpreted above. They are not so much the creature of this world as the imaginative principles of such creatures. The stars are without a name because the fecundity of the creative principle outstrips our capacity to name all its possible creations. Keats' poem allows us to perceive how the union of the self with the supreme principle

---

19. B. Blackstone, *The Consecrated Urn*, passim (London: Longmans Green 1959).

of consciousness releases the enormous energies of creation, Macrocosmically these energies generate the Universe; microcosmically, the work of art.

Again, there can be no doubt that one of the elements in the story of Apuleius which most attracted Keats was the tension which the story develops between sacred and profane love. This is one of the two or three major themes in *Endymion* and it is also a major theme in *The Eve of St. Agnes*. In the very last lines of the *Ode to Psyche* Keats achieves a resolution of this tension as successful as any in his work. In Apuleius' story the resolution is the taking of Psyche to heaven and her becoming fully divinized as the wife of Cupid and the mother of Pleasure. But in Keats' poem the resolution is different. At the very end of the poem Cupid and Psyche set up house once again as they had at the beginning of Apuleius' story, but this time there is no restriction upon their looking on each other with their eyes in the full light. Indeed, the light is now the very means by which Cupid can be guided through the open window to where his Psyche awaits him. The torch and the window are sexual symbols. They are also metaphors for the poem as a meditative technique by which the self can return to a full understanding of its own consciousness. But finally and primarily, the bright torch and the window symbolize the way in which Keats can accommodate the fullest physical sexuality to the most perfect intellectual realization. In the infinite self rejoicing, to use Coleridge's phrase, nothing whatsoever is forbidden.[20]

Despite a reversal of roles the overall pictures provided by Apuleius' fable and Keats' poem are very similar. Both are concerned with self discovery through a process of introspection. For both, Cupid's palace is a symbol of the creative powers of the intellect or imagination. Yet from another point of view there is a much greater difference between them than any I have so far discussed.

In one respect Apuleius' fable achieves nothing of what Keats achieves in the *Ode to Psyche*. The fable is the residue or precipitate of the rapture which it describes, while in some extraordinary way Keats' poem is the rapture itself. The poem is the bright torch and

20. S. T. Coleridge, "Essay on Method", Section II, Essay X, *The Friend*.

the open window by which the self reunites with the spirit. It is these things because it is itself the moment of reunion. In some way the *Ode to Psyche* narrows the gap between vision and expression to vanishing point. This is possible, in this case and no other, because the vision is purely intellectual, a matter of self reflection and not of things. Consciousness is not itself an object of experience. The subject who describes it, the act of description and what is described are one and the same. This One is the ultimate goal of desire to which the whole creation aspires. The poem holds us in this union for its entire length, rising to a climax in the last stanza. The world beyond the poem, if it exists, exists for the poem's sake and not otherwise.

It has become unusual to celebrate the interior life and a spiritualized natural world. To my ear this is a defiant poem which insists that the inner world, inner truth, the *unio mystica* is the only goal worth pursuing. In this poem Keats is with Blake at his most strident. It is a missionary poem for a spiritual vision which was in the view of both poets rapidly closing in their heartland. Insofar as the *Ode to Psyche* triumphantly reasserts the purpose of the inward life and search in its purest form, it is to be ranked with Henry Vaughan's *The World*, say, or Wordsworth's *Recollection Ode*. Since the vision which Keats enacts here is the equivalent of Plato's Vision of the Good, or the apprehension of Parmenidean Being, we should rank Keats in his poetry as a supremely successful intellectual, one perfected and initiated from this point onwards. The *Ode to Psyche* is Keats' masterpiece. From now on he is a light to himself:

I see, and sing, by my own eyes inspired.

9

A MANIFESTO
FOR THE HUMANITIES

Why study the Humanities? The proper reply to this question in the first instance is that one should study the Humanities for their own sake and for no other reason whatsoever. One does it not as a means to some other good, not even because it is enjoyable, but as an end or good in itself. This is not to say that the study of the Humanities does not provide benefits to oneself and others, only that these benefits are incidental to the good which is the study. To speak of these other benefits in the first instance is to derogate the study, turning it from being an end to being merely the means. Of course, this reply is not likely to satisfy the questioner, who does not understand that the study is a good in itself. If this were understood, there would be no need for the question. But for all that, this is the proper reply in the first instance.

Furthermore, the reply can be followed by a demonstration of how vital the distinction between means and ends is. For example, it is increasingly the practice to quantify the cost of certain specified illnesses and kinds of accident, not merely by counting the number of victims but in dollar terms. From here we could conceivably proceed seriously to ask ourselves such questions as "What is the point of being fit if there is no money in it?' Now this question is patently absurd to anyone who knows what a good thing fitness is. In the same way the asking for some good from the study of the Humanities beyond the study itself looks absurd to those who know what the Humanities are. And one can point to the risks that follow upon the conversion of ends into means in general. We live at a time when a great many people find their lives to be meaningless. The fewer the activities and associations which people regard as ends in themselves, the poorer the quality of their lives.

Duty

A similar case can be made out from a slightly different point of view. The study of the Humanities is both a good in itself and also a duty incumbent upon the people of each generation. Each generation has the power, but not the right, to neglect this duty. Each receives the bulk of its literature, history, art from the generation before. This inheritance is inalienable. No generation has the right to choose whether to accept it or not. It must remain 'in the family' indefinitely. Not only is there a duty to study these works of the past, there is also a duty to transmit them to the next generation. And there are still other duties: to improve the conditions of these works; to discover more of them; to expound their meanings; and to add to them condign works by contemporary artists and authors.

There are several ways of regarding these duties. They may be understood simply as that, not as duties to anyone but as duties incumbent on the people of each generation without further qualification. Or they may be regarded as duties to parents or even to ancestors in return for their gifts of life and education. Or as duties to descendants in the same way as some people suppose that each generation has a duty to its descendants to conserve the natural environment. The Humanities, I feel, occupy a special place in relation to these duties. All the intellectual achievements of the past should be studied and handed on, but most of all the Humanities because they are, in part, the oldest. It would be a dreadful thing if we with all our wealth should fail in this duty where our ancestors have succeeded, despite every hardship, from the time of Homer till now. In the eleventh book of Homer's *Odyssey* Odysseus evokes the ghosts of the dead. When we stand with him at the ditch of blood and confront the multitudinous ghosts of the dead, we stare into the depths of an antiquity already ancient by Homer's time. This moment is one image of tradition in culture.

The argument that the study of the Humanities is a duty is like the argument that it is a good in itself in this respect: it brings in no considerations extrinsic to the study itself in order to make its point. To grant the truth of these arguments is also to grant that there is no other way than by studying the Humanities that this good can be achieved, this duty fulfilled. With extrinsic considerations, on the other hand, it is always possible that the benefit achieved through the study could be achieved in some other way. That said, we may turn to the various extrinsic considerations. But first we must dispose of a spurious argument which will otherwise drag at our heels.

Cultural Relativism

The relativist argument is that cultures may be described, even measured, but they cannot be judged. On this view any cultural order is a more or less closed system with its own codes and values, and every judgement belongs within one or other of these systems and never outside it. There is no point of view from which the merits and debits of two different systems may be conclusively weighed against each other. Any such judgement must be made on the basis of values which belong within one or other of the two systems, or within a third system which is necessarily as limited in its point of view as the other two. The cultures of an undiscovered African tribe, of Athens in the fifth century before Christ, of a medieval Italian city, of Australia in the twenty-first century are all equally valid expressions of the human spirit, and there is nothing to choose between them.[1]

At first sight this is attractive. It absolves us from having to enquire into the details of different cultures before we pass judgement on them. They are all equally valid from the start. But it follows from this that there is nothing to choose between a culture in which the Humanities are studied and one in which they are not. Unless we dispose of this we cannot proceed. In my experience cul-

---

1. Roger Trigg, *Understanding Social Sciences* (London: Blackwell 1985). "The emphasis laid on the incommensurability of theories by Feyerabend, as well as Kuhn, develops into a position where theories or traditions set their own standards of rationality and are immune to criticism from outside."

tural relativists are not persuaded by counter examples. They account it toughness of mind to accommodate the most ludicrous consequences of their theory. For them a barbarous tyranny is no worse than constitutional democracy provided only that it belongs in context. They must therefore be opposed at their own level, the theoretical. In general, they make an absolute claim that no claim about culture can be absolute.

What of this claim? Does it proceed from within a culture or not? If not, then by its own account it is groundless. But if it does proceed from within a culture, then it is part of that culture's debate about culture and must take its place within the range of positions which make up that debate. As an argument to end all arguments about culture, it turns out to be no argument at all. Or, to put it another way, if there is no absolute position beyond all cultures, then a position within a culture is as absolute a position as there is. But such a position is no more absolute than any other such position. It has to be argued.

Let us now consider the claim that there is nothing to choose between a culture in which the Humanities are studied and one in which they are not. It is not difficult to show how this is wrong. To do this I need first to develop the notion of cultural self-sufficiency, the self-sufficiency of the understanding and imagination. By this I do not mean mere independence of mind though this is certainly part of it. Consider for example the reading of a novel and the watching of a film of that novel. The reader of the novel has to imagine the scenes, characters and events which the novel describes in a way that the watcher of a film does not. The reading of the novel is the product of this interaction between reader and novel and it is in large part the reader's own work. The reader enters into an active possession of the book. Certain subtle faculties are brought into play. Play indeed affords another example. Compare two children, one playing with plastic soldiers, the other playing with pebbles or twigs which he or she imagines to be soldiers. This second child can play soldiers almost anywhere, the first may not be so adaptive. This power to amuse ourselves with our own thoughts is one of the powers which the study of the Humanities develops.

If we compare a more traditional society with our own, we can see that the new technologies of entertainment in the twentieth century have made a great difference in this regard. Television, for the most part, does not develop the powers of its spectators so much as it hypnotizes them. Among certain traditional peoples on the other hand, even reading is held in low esteem. No one is regarded as knowing a book just from having read it many times. A book is known when it is known by heart. Until then one can only be said to know of a book.[2] An illiterate tribal elder with a full knowledge of the tribe's mythology and ritual is an awesome figure even by our standards.

A culture should not be considered merely as the total of beliefs and practices of a number at a given time and place. This is one meaning of the term, but culture is also, and more literally, the tending of living creatures so that they grow and develop to their limits. In this sense we can talk of better and worse cultures. There are many different methods of development and many different directions in which to develop. But there is not usually much doubt in anyone's mind about whether there has been some development of a person's faculties or none at all. If the Humanities were not studied, and no alternative means of development found, our culture would suffer. And we would be thinking so in those circumstances as well as in these.

Self-Enlargement

Self-sufficiency of the understanding and imagination is valuable in itself. It is also a means by which people assimilate themselves fully to their cultural inheritance. To this end self-sufficiency is usually indispensable. What a cultural inheritance typically does, it seems, is to realize a range of possibilities latent in the experience of the people who study it. Assimilation to it brings about a marriage between what people know of themselves and what they are. The characteristic feeling is one of self-enlargement. No one who has taught the Humanities can have completely avoided the gratitude of

2. For examples, see A. Coomaraswamy, *The Bugbear of Literacy* (Middlesex: Perennial Books, 1979).

students who mistakenly attribute to the teacher their own discovery of new worlds in the works they are studying. Doors, they say, have been opened. In some cases these latent possibilities are extraordinarily pressing, in individuals and sometimes even in a majority of the people attending a single class. As with rain on a desert, there are plants ready to spring up everywhere. One can feel the thirst in the ground.

This phenomenon is easy to describe but hard to explain. In a famous essay T. S. Eliot talks of the mind of Europe, which is more important than any private mind and which comprises all the works of the European tradition.[3] It is to this larger mind that any new poet must conform. Each new work looks back in a new way at the works of the past. This is why the Cantos of Ezra Pound begin with a translation of Odysseus' encounter with the dead. There is also the genius of language, a personality which goes beyond all users of the language past and present, a storehouse of possibilities. In these two notions there are some common elements: in each the greater entity is a unity and the minds or speech of people somehow belong to it whether this is acknowledged or not. It is a whole of which all the speakers or thinkers are parts. Students of the Humanities have a sense of some such being as this and it matters to them. Others either lack the sense or do not acknowledge it, as they do not acknowledge a duty to preserve the works which we have inherited from generations of our ancestors.[4] It is, I believe, the encounter with such a being which gives the feeling of self-enlargement to students of the Humanities, and the need of it which is their thirst.

In more normal times it would be taken for granted that this feeling of self-enlargement represented an actual enlargement of the students' sympathies. The great diversity of points of view, ways of thinking, experiences and relationships encountered in a study of the Humanities would be thought to render the student more humane and broad-minded. 'Nothing human do I consider foreign to me', the Roman playwright said. On this view the study of the

---

3. T. S. Eliot, *Selected Essays*, "Tradition and the Individual Talent", 1932, Faber.
4. For a comparable view of tradition see Alasdair MacIntyre, *After Virtue*, 1981, Duckworth.

Humanities makes the societies in which they are studied more harmonious. But these are not normal times. The history of Western Europe in the twentieth century has convinced some people that the study of the Humanities no longer achieves enough in this regard, if it ever did. When Germany, one of the most cultivated nations in Europe, organized the death camps, humane culture had failed. An Italian journalist describes how Frank, the Nazi governor of Poland, played Chopin on the piano to his guests after dinner, then took them out to shoot Jewish children escaping past the walls of the Warsaw ghetto.[5] People who had studied the Humanities at the highest level engaged actively in mass murder. 'Why did humanistic traditions and models of conduct prove so fragile a barrier against political bestiality?' George Steiner asks.[6]

For all that, it has to be said that Hitler came to power after nearly twenty years of continuous disaster for the German people. Nobody, I think, would ever seriously claim that the study of the Humanities would preserve the humanity of a nation under any circumstances for any period of time. We do not reject medicine because some patients die despite their doctors' efforts. The Nazis regarded the Humanities, as they had been taught, with suspicion. They wished to purge the inherited tradition as well as to alter the direction which the arts had taken in their own time. There was a long exodus of intellectuals of all persuasions from Germany when Hitler came to power and many more who stayed were murdered. These are good reasons for supposing that the Humanities as they had been taught were a serious obstruction to Nazi ideology, and that they required reorganization before they suited the purposes of the regime. "When I hear the word 'culture', I reach for my revolver" one Nazi leader is reported to have said. Still more significant is Hitler's comment that without the radio he would not have come to power.

5. Curzio Malaparte, *Kaputt*, 1958, Redman.
6. George Steiner, *In Bluebeard's Castle*, 1971, Faber.

Mechanical Reproduction

Film, television and radio, together with other ways of recording sound, have profoundly altered our relations to the material of the Humanities. At first it was believed that the study of the Humanities would benefit greatly from the wide availability of these technologies. It was an ideal of their producers that they would increase people's access to the great works of the past, but little thought was given to how they would modify the relationships between the works and those who observed them.

At first, no doubt, the habits inculcated by more traditional disciplines of study, reinforced by the awe with which the new machines were regarded, allowed these works something of the same attention which they had always been accorded. Even so, there was always the danger that the attention would be diverted from the works themselves to the technology which made them available, a diversion which neatly placed the student of a work in a position superior to its creator if the creator had lived before the machine was invented. It has since become clear that these machines may be used to undermine all the habits needed for the proper appreciation of these works. These habits are replaceable by one single, all pervading attitude of the mind, interest. In the new world of sights and sounds presented to us by the reproductive technologies of the twentieth century, it is interest most often which provides people with direction or with the illusion of direction. Great stories, symphonies, the finest paintings jostle each other for our interest, which we bestow on them with a momentary enthusiasm and then pass on.

At the very least the study of these works requires that students give each in turn their undivided attention for a considerable time over and over again. Almost always more than this is required, a study of the historical period and its assumptions out of which the work came. In the first instance serious students approach each work on the understanding that they must cease to be who they are in order to become as it is. Only when they have been sympathetically absorbed may they usefully criticize. They think of the work as a kind of teacher which develops the intelligence of those who study it, not as material on which to exercise an intelligence already formed. Nothing less than devotion is required. Interest is the reverse of all this. The work is enjoyed for its attractiveness only. The labour which created it sets off the idleness of an observer whose commitment to it may be no more than the casual turning of a knob. The delights of the millennia are offered up to this voluptuary for whom they form not a succession but a single, simultaneous moment. The iconography of the works, the doctrines which they embody, are not just unknown but unsuspected, as though the artists of Abu Simbel and those of the Bauhaus differed merely in point of style. Unaffected by what it observes, interest moves round and round in an unbreakable circuit, never escaping its own limitations whatever its object.[7]

The new technologies are often abused but they do not have to be. There are ways in which the film of a novel elicits less of a contribution from those who watch it than does the novel from its readers, but this is not to say that there is no place for the cinema, nor yet for films of novels. In some cases a new technology considerably improves our ability to concentrate on the works it mediates. It is often an advantage to listen to a difficult string quartet in solitude, rather than hear it live among an audience. Color photography and the slide projector have made paintings available for study on a scale and with an accuracy never before known. To lose the aura of the original painting is a price worth paying for this. The new technologies can be what their first exponents dreamt they would be. Far more often they are the means of undermining the works which they were supposed to serve. The difference between use and abuse is study. The power for good or evil of these technologies entails a duty upon these societies which have them to ensure that works of art are given the respect which is appropriate to them. The availability of these technologies presents a new and compelling reason for the study of the Humanities. And students of the

7. Laura (Riding) Jackson, "Interest", *The Massachusetts Review*, 1982, Autumn. "There has been more and more interest expended by human beings on more and more, and this could be how human existence exhausts itself in itself—should nothing or no-one stop them from living as parasites upon their intelligence, it dying of them, they dying of it, dead."

Humanities are particularly well fitted to provide these technologies
with a content worth communicating.

Wisdom

Plato, the founder of the Academy, has left us a striking picture of
education. The world of nature he compares to an underground
cave in which we are all prisoners, seeing only shadows cast on a wall
by a great fire. The teacher comes down into the cave to free us, by
leading us up to the world above where we no longer see shadows
but things as they really are. When we have seen all this we should
return to help those still imprisoned in the cave. This picture of education illustrates the twin principles of detachment and transcendence: education is not concerned with worldly advantages but with
a reality beyond nature. Detachment, the ideal of disinterested and
dispassionate teaching and research, has been a largely undisputed
principle of Western education from Plato's time onwards. Transcendence has been the achievement of Western education in its
greatest periods, and an ideal throughout its history.

It is hard to judge how far the changes through which we are now
passing threaten these principles. So far as detachment is concerned, all that matters is whether the men and women who undertake study and teaching do so to pursue knowledge for its own sake
and from the desire to help others. These seem less and less the
avowed goals of the great professions. Scales grading the likely earnings of graduates from different degree course are especially repel-
lent in this regard. In the last twenty years or more natural scientists
have been pressed to forsake pure research, research for its own
sake, in order to concentrate on the making of discoveries which
will turn a profit. The irony is that pure research is probably the
more effective way of making such discoveries since nobody can
know beforehand where the profitable breakthrough will come.

As for transcendence, the maintaining of this ideal was traditionally the task of Theology among the faculties and disciplines of
higher education. With the gradual disappearance of Theology
from modern institutions of learning, this responsibility also
devolved upon the Humanities, particularly the study of poetry and

the History of Philosophy. It need not have come to the Humanities only. In the same passage in which Plato gives his picture of education he explains how the path which leads from the cave to the upper world is the study of mathematics. Mathematics accustoms the mind to the contemplation of invisibles, so preparing it for the intellectual vision of the supreme principle. But Plato was himself more than half a poet and it is now most often through the study of poetry that a student encounters the possibility of an intellectual approach to that principle. But if the History of Philosophy and the study of such poetry were themselves to disappear from institutions of learning in the West, that would mean that the Academy would have ceased to exist. The name might linger for a while, but the thing itself would be gone. As much could be said of institutional education in general. I do not suggest this because I think it will happen, but because the contemplation of education without the Humanities helps to show the power of their presence.

10

PHILOSOPHY
IN A DARK AGE

Philosophy as a discipline is a range of competing theories concerning the possibility and nature of human knowledge—ethical, scientific, aesthetic, spiritual. There is another sense of the term philosophy: a Thomist, a Marxist, an empiricist might each of them start a speech with the words "What Philosophy teaches is…" and then proceed to give an account of their own doctrines, contradicting the views of the other two. In this sense philosophy is not a range of competing theories, but the one among them which the speaker believes. And the proponent of a philosophy in this limited sense might have a different view from the proponents of other such philosophies as to what the discipline as a whole should include.

Here is a passage from Plato's *Republic*. Socrates is speaking:

…other manikins, observing that the place is unoccupied and full of fine terms and pretensions, just as men escape from prison to take sanctuary in temples, so these gentlemen joyously bound away from the mechanical arts to philosophy, those that are most cunning in their little craft. For in comparison with the other arts the prestige of philosophy even in her present low estate retains a superior dignity, and this is the ambition and aspiration of the multitude of pretenders unfit by nature, whose souls are bowed and mutilated by their vulgar occupations even as their bodies are marred by their arts and crafts. Is not that inevitable?

Quite so, he said.

Is not the picture which they present, I said, precisely that of a little bald-headed tinker who has made money and just been freed from bonds and had a bath and is wearing a new garment and has got himself up like a bridegroom and is about to marry his master's daughter who has fallen into poverty and abandonment?[1]

This passage exemplifies the second sense given to the term philosophy above. Here a proponent of a particular philosophy, let us say Pythagoreanism, is urging that this philosophy is properly philosophy and that the other theories are vulgar pretenders to that title. Socrates supposes that philosophy is a science already in existence and is only now in danger of an unworthy union with mechanics. Since Pythagoras is credited with having coined the term philosophy and since the doctrines of Plato are largely assimilable to those of the Pythagoreans, we may suppose that Socrates is speaking here as a Pythagorean, as a member of a self-proclaimed philosophical tradition.

In the discipline of philosophy Platonism, as we have come to call it, is just one theory of knowledge among others. From the point of view of Platonists old and new, it is, of course, the one. And modern Platonists have two good arguments for supposing that it is the one. The first argument is that for the greater part of Western history as preserved, Platonism is the prevailing doctrine, though often tempered by Aristotelianism. The line is from Plato, to Aristotle, Plotinus, Proclus, Augustine, Boethius, Pseudo Dionysius, Aquinas, Ficino, Thomas Taylor and more recently. René Guénon. The second argument is that among Western theories the doctrines of Platonism most closely correspond to the doctrines of other traditions. The Platonic exponents of this universalism are Philojudaeus, Porphyry, Pico della Mirandola and Ananda Coomaraswamy.

The fact that Platonism is a very long lasting and very widespread doctrine does not make it true. In the discipline of philosophy, unlike democracy, it is not how many people believe something but whether they are right to believe it that matters. On the other hand

1. Plato, *Republic*, 495C–E.

it is a major step to reject the accumulated testimony of all those intellectuals over many ages and across many nations. But this, of course, is precisely what modernism is. But modernism did not arise from a refuted Platonism. To be sure, John Locke devoted the first chapters of the *Essay Concerning Human Understanding* to a demolishing of the notion that we are born with certain ideas. But though he had been a lecturer in Greek at Oxford, Locke did not feel the need to controvert Plato's accounts of innate ideas, even though Plato was the Classical exponent of the theory. Locke does not mention Plato. In the *Theaetetus* Plato seriously criticized the theory that all human knowledge is derived from sense perception, Locke's own belief, but neither does Locke mention this.

A similar but much more striking omission may be found in the treatment of Locke's great contemporary, Isaac Newton. There still exist two autograph versions of an essay by Newton in which he compared his theory of gravity to certain understandings of the Pythagoreans and the ancient Atomists. Newton argued that the inverse square law was known to the Pythagoreans as the principle governing the tuning of strings: the note one octave higher than a given note may be achieved either by halving the length of the string or by quadrupling the tension on the string; the note one and a half octaves higher is achieved by trisecting the string or increasing its tension ninefold. Newton believed that the Pythagoreans transferred this ratio to the heavens, so that what he called gravity was for them the principle of attunement or harmony among the stars of the solar system. Newton relied on the late Roman author Macrobius for what he wrote about the Pythagoreans and both of them may well have been wrong historically. But what Newton wrote about his own theory and the ancients has been ignored for centuries, because unpublished till the 1960s. This was the fate of Newton's *Classical Scholia*. From Locke's essay onwards, there seems to have been a tendency to sequester the new science and the new philosophy from their links to the past. Locke told how he and his friends tried to establish some foundations of the human understanding in an entirely original way, totally rejecting the scholastic confusions of the past. Locke bypassed the ghosts, he did not lay them. Newton faced them but his encounter was shelved.

In the eighteenth and nineteenth centuries Locke's influence was mitigated by the classical learning of the English Renaissance on the one side and by Christian theology on the other. But in the twentieth century these mitigating factors have largely disappeared. It is common now for students trained in philosophy in the Anglosphere to suppose that the discipline of philosophy turns on twentieth century forms of empiricism, linguistic analysis, existentialism and relativism. Since such updating is exactly what has happened in every other discipline, this change in the discipline of philosophy has gone largely unremarked.

And so we come in our turn to that little bald-headed tinker. In the *Republic* he was got up like a bridegroom to marry his master's daughter; he was a figure of fun, a butt for upper-class scorn. In our time he has become more terrifying. For now he holds the keys to the Academy itself. As Plato said of his time, so in ours the name of philosophy retains a certain lustre. Consider the extended uses of 'Doctor of Philosophy'. Philosophy is still an essential discipline for every serious enquirer, but such students who come to the modern Academy may find the experience painful. An aspiring student of philosophy who is driven by the impulse which Plato describes, an inchoate love of beauty and goodness beyond all their forms in experience, such a student often suffers under the authority of the professionals who now occupy Plato's place. What we call the spirit and Plato called the intellect is in need of nurturing. Hence the Academy. But institutions which are advertised as nurses of the intellect may do the very opposite. Of course, Philosophy departments should teach many theories of knowledge. But they must teach Platonism, and teach it well. This is less and less the case.

Bad enough for the Platonizing or Christian philosophy student, this failure is far more deadly to those who frustrate them. From the spiritual point of view the mishandling of the intellectual impulse by those who have a duty to foster it, is a considerable offence. And in these cases the offence is authorized, sponsored, enabled by the institution in which it happens. So guilt for the offence must be borne by that institution's most senior officers. They cannot benefit from the reflected glory of the institution and at the same time escape responsibility for the undermining of its most sacred function. It would be much safer for them if they abandoned the names Academic and philosophy altogether.

With the decline of Platonism has come the mutation of University Marxism into Postmodernism. To the Marxist, culture and belief were expressions of the relations between classes, of the economic order. For the Postmodernist, truth itself has become a rhetorical structure, a ruse for the gaining of influence: learning and education are not primarily matters of knowledge at all but of power, the kind of power exercised by one person over another. This ascent beyond truth rather embarrasses the empiricist and the language analyst. In *A Farewell to Arts* David Stove described how there was no dealing with the feminist revolution of his time by any of his canons of reason or argument. But the notion that social and political power is the ultimate reality, and everything else reflects this power, is a theme frequently discussed in Plato's Dialogues. With Callicles in the *Gorgias*, with Thrasymachus in *The Republic*, Socrates carefully fillets this theory of power. Socrates' stance against power theory was the core of his philosophical career in Athens, as Plato presents it. The crucial distinction was between philosophy, in the limited sense of his philosophy, and oratory. To Socrates democratic oratory was a form of flattery. He seems to have thought the Athenian parliament a jury of children empanelled to judge between a fast-food chef and a dietician. Orators need only persuade their audiences of their wisdom and statesmanship; philosophers must actually be wise. When public opinion is the decider, this great distinction tends to blur, and power theory is one of the characteristic forms of that blurring. The decline of Platonism in the University has made the re-invention of Athenian sophistry, in the form of Postmodernism, much too easy.

Then there are the Freudians who claim to deconstruct us along sexual lines. The energies in which they deal were well known to Plato who, like Freud, recognized them in the Tragedies. For Plato, those energies characteristically erupted in the tyrant, the unhappiest of all human types. Plato knew what Oedipus learnt, that those energies were much better left entirely alone. In Sophocles' play, the prophet insisted to Oedipus that the plague afflicting Thebes was preferable to discovering its cause. Freud prefaced his *Introductory*

Lectures on Psychoanalysis with this line from Virgil's *Aeneid*:

If I cannot sway the Gods, I will move Acheron.[2]

Freud did move Hell, and we should heed his self-revelation here. Where Pythagoreanism and Platonism are means to spiritual integration. Freudianism promotes the dissolution of the psyche and is as purely counter-philosophical as it is possible to be.

Plato drew the line at this vileness. But across the same line he welcomed the power-theorists, mechanists, empiricists and materialists. They are the characters of his dialogues, the atmosphere against which his wings gained their traction. I can think of no other philosopher who consistently represents his opponents' arguments as brilliantly as Plato does. But Plato's eminence in the oldest phase of our tradition, and his aristocratic values, make it hard for us not to think of him as some archetypal conservative from long before the era of the common man. Historically he is already post-democratic and his philosophical preoccupations have been formed in the democratic maelstrom of his youth and early manhood. Socrates speaks of philosophy as an established institution fallen on hard times. But our notion of that philosophy comes largely from Plato himself, who is already armed head to foot against democratic deviations from it. So Plato is, as it were, some way ahead of us if the historical process repeats itself. He is in the future. But as an influential ancient philosopher, he is already deeply imbedded in the culture now. The greater part of the philosophy discipline in modern times is more or less explicitly anti-Platonic, from Bacon and Locke onwards. Plato has been the centre of an anti-philosophical centrifuge for a long time already. So our own post-democratic philosophers, if we develop so far, will need to surpass Plato's legacy just as Derrida, for one, has surpassed the Sophists. Derrida's relativism is profoundly informed by a knowledge of philosophy from many ages, as it touches also on apophatic and nominalist themes.

Let us indulge our wildest imaginings. Let us dream that this essay or one like it is widely published and unanimously deplored in the so called media. The universities confer and it is decided that

2. Virgil, *Aeneid*, VII, 312.

they will no longer teach Platonism because it has always declared itself to be anti-democratic and because it is insufficiently respectful of other people's opinions. This is consonant, they say, with the general shift in educational theory over the last two generations, from the notion that the goal was to provide a traditional upper-class education to everyone who could manage it, to the notion that such an education was irredeemably compromised by its classist, sexist and racist assumptions. No matter that Plato promoted the education of women to the highest levels and condoned Socrates' homophilia. His antiquity alone is enough to condemn him. The edict goes out and the philosophy departments make the necessary adjustment. What a marvellous thing that would be! Students of real intellectual worth would no longer be attracted to the universities by false advertising; university teachers and administrators would no longer be compromised by the dangerous hypocrisy of calling themselves Academics; and philosophy itself, in that limited, Platonic sense, would be free of all the flummery of university doctorates in philosophy which bear no relation to the discipline. Numbers of intellectuals have long been promoting Platonism outside the universities, where the best work in philosophy was done in the twentieth century. In the event of the exclusion of Platonism from the universities, a powerful milieu of true philosophy, such as preceded the founding of the first Academy, is ready and waiting.

Plato's writings are powerfully relevant to our own philosophical debates but this alone does not make him indispensable. Plato matters more than this because he determined the goal of philosophy, the target at which it aims. That is the Idea of the Good, the unhypothesized beginning, union while we yet live with the source and principle of everything. We are to reach this goal by an ever sharper and more intense 'thinking of thinking' for which no faith is required. Plato offers in detail a purely *intellectual* transcendence and it is this which makes him indispensable. As a result and incidentally, his work was almost equally adaptable to both of the two major religious dispensations of our Western epoch, the Classical and the Christian. His work was one of the most substantial continuities between them. In the medieval universities which followed Boethius in their Platonic curriculum, the transcendental goal of theology and philosophy was the Beatific Vision. The great doctors such as Aquinas and Bonaventura were thought angelic. Today Academy and University have set their sights much lower and the greatest service the Platonist or Christian can do them is to remind them constantly of their present inferiority. Their many conflicting 'cultures', the disarray of their disciplines, could never have created an intellectual institution by themselves.

11

METAPHYSICS OF
PROFESSIONAL LIFE

Ethicists and moral philosophers try to determine what is ethical and what is just in difficult, and in many cases quite novel, dilemmas. Technological change continually generates new dilemmas of this kind. But even if we could find satisfactory resolutions to all these dilemmas, that could never be the end of the matter. All the ethics in the world will not help us until we find a satisfactory answer to this one question first: why be ethical or just anyway?

With this almost indecent question Professor Anderson of Sydney University made a long habit of dropping moralists in their tracks from the 1920s through to the 1960s. Quite rightly, Anderson saw his question 'Why be ethical?' as a defining question of philosophy as a discipline. He adduced Socrates as another like himself who saw his professional life as the asking of such impossible questions of everyone at all times. Like Socrates, Anderson insisted on an answer, and when it was not forthcoming or was demonstrably inadequate, he took this as proof that the moral claims of his target had no basis whatsoever. Like Socrates, this made Anderson a deeply unpopular man in many circles.

But neither Anderson nor Socrates ever exerted quite the pressure on their victims which Plato describes in the *Republic*. Here Socrates himself is put under interrogation by two of his students, Adeimantus and Glaucon. Socrates himself is forced to answer the question 'why be just?' His interrogators make quite clear what they want from him: proof that being just, in itself, is more in ones interests than being unjust. And then they add the dreadful rider: 'under any circumstances'. Let the unjust man in our comparison, they tell

Socrates, be a master criminal, never caught and universally respected as a model citizen. Let the just man be universally reviled as a moral monster, though completely innocent. Let him be whipped and racked, let his eyes be burnt out with branding irons and let him finally be crucified to death. Prove to us that this just man, simply because he is just, is nonetheless better off than our universally honoured criminal.

I will attempt the proof which Adeimantus and Glaucon demanded of Socrates that day in the Peiraeus. I undertake this philosophical challenge. I will not meet it in quite the ways which Socrates did. I will not be proving that that the just man is exactly 729 times better off than the unjust man, as Socrates proves to the satisfaction of Adeimantus and Glaucon by the end of the *Republic*. But I will consider that greatest proof of all which Socrates offered by cheerfully allowing himself to be executed for the sake of his vocation. My proof will be rather more poetic than Socrates in the *Republic*, but it will meet the challenge posed by Adeimantus and Glaucon squarely, in all its horror.

The title of this essay is concerned with professional life and I will consider the question 'why be ethical?' in the context of the professions. In doing this I will in any case be following Socrates' procedure in the *Republic* and Aristotle's at the beginning of his *Nicomachean Ethics*. There Aristotle begins by distinguishing between a flute player and a good flute player. More authoritatively still, I will be following Homer who is the supremely wise teacher in the Greek tradition. Homer has much to say about professions and crafts of every kind, but his great contribution to the topic is his presentation of the professions and crafts as divine. For Homer, what we now think of as the forms of human work are what the Gods do on Olympus. By this simple transfer, Homer establishes the fundamental character of these forms of work: they are the activities of the spirit in eternity. Now, of course, we rush to say here that Homer's Gods behaved this way because they are simply human projections of human activities. But Homer saw it differently.

Homer's peculiar view of divine and human work has an upside and a downside. The upside is that if we believe it, then we discover that we are, in our workaday worlds, already very much closer to heaven than we had realized. When we work we are cooperating in the various forms taken by the divine energy in all eternity. This raises our human experiences at work far above the sense of the human we derive from Christian teaching, say. The downside is that this view may demean the divine in our eyes. For it is part of the definition of the divine that it be utterly self-sufficient. But the function of the crafts and professions is to supply what we lack. If then the Gods on Olympus need doctors and weavers and metallurgists, they are obviously inferior in this respect to the Judaeo-Christian God who has no such needs. But the Christian God, too, made heaven and earth.

Homer's Gods have a house doctor on Olympus. His name is Paieon. He cures Hades, the God of the dead, when Hades comes to Olympus in agony, with an arrow in his shoulder from Hercules. Paieon treats him with anaesthetic herbs on the wound. Paieon does the same for Ares, God of War, when Diomedes wounds him in the lower abdomen with a spear. Ares bellowed as loudly as ten thousand warriors with the shock and pain, but Paieon heals him quickly because Ares is after all a God. He heals him as quickly as it takes fig juice to curdle white milk, a striking image of how firm flesh is made from wet wounds. In fact the Gods hardly seem to need Paieon for they are generally expert enough at healing each other. But they certainly need Hephaestus to build their palaces for them, Apollo and the Muses to make their music.

Are there law and lawyers on Olympus? Certainly not in any written form. As for an oral law, it appears that force alone determines how power is shared among the Gods. When Aphrodite commits adultery with Ares in her husband Hephaestus' bed, Hephaestus traps them both under a golden net. He then calls the other Gods to witness the trapped lovers and refuses to release them from their public humiliation. He demands compensation for his wooing gifts for Aphrodite, not only from Ares, whom he fears will welsh on any agreement once he is freed, but from Poseidon himself. To spare Aphrodite and Ares any further shame, Poseidon promises to pay whatever is right if Ares defaults. So there is clearly a sense of what is right among the Gods, but Hephaestus knows that he can only ensure just treatment for himself for as long as he keeps the lovers in his net. If he is to let them go, he must have a publicly spoken promise from Poseidon to pay the compensation if necessary.

In the *Homeric Hymn to Demeter*, Demeter caused a dreadful famine which nearly destroyed humankind. She was furious at Hades' abduction of her daughter. Zeus is in a dilemma. He himself has permitted Hades to take the girl and he cannot go back on his word. But he must either break that word or lose the human race. He arbitrates cunningly by giving the girl back to her mother for two-thirds of the year and to Hades for one third. Her sojourn with Hades is winter, her return to her mother is spring. The compromise which he adjudicates is the cause of the seasons.

Zeus cannot go back on his word. In Homer's poetry it appears that this one limitation constrains him. But Zeus is also said to be bound by fate which he may bend a little but which he cannot override. The question is whether this fate is anything more than his own previously ratified decisions. If fate is no more than what Zeus himself has already decided, then clearly there is, in a sense, a body of Law on Olympus and the other Gods seem to know of the Law and they argue with Zeus and with each other as to exactly what it entails.

So the Gods practise medicine and argue law, in this limited sense, among themselves. Athena weaves, Hephaestus builds and works at his forge, the Muses compose verses, the Graces dance. As for the hard sciences, we need only remember the problem posed by Apollo through his oracle at Delphi, when he demanded that the Greeks exactly double the size of his cubic altar on Delos. There is no way of doubling the size of a cube by means of ratios, which is how the Greeks practised mathematics. Even wheat farming which was not needed by the Gods who do not eat our food, the Gods nonetheless sponsored in the figure of Demeter, Ceres. She it was who first taught the people of Eleusis to till the earth. Why did the Greeks think that the Gods too practised the crafts and professions?

Let us forget for a while that the Olympians themselves use many products of their labours. Do Gods work? By definition Gods have no future nor past. They are fully realized, so they have no potential in them to have become other than they were or to become other than they are. From our point of view Gods cannot act or work because they are not in time. But from another point of view they cannot do other than act to the limit of their powers because they have no potential but are fully realized. We mortals on the other hand are at a single point in a series or continuum, a temporal sequence with more and less distant moments beyond now. And our actions are rarely if ever as perfectly finished and effective as those of the Gods.

In their discriminations between the many powers of the Absolute, the Greeks worshipped Gods as the essential energies of everything else that existed. Even the minerals in the ground owed their various properties to the planetary Gods. The planets themselves in their complex, invariant courses move both inside and outside time, since they are the instrument of time. Why did the planets move in their courses? Because they too were divine intelligences in rapt contemplation and perfect activity, whose wisdom was demonstrated by the predictability of their movements. According to Plato, it was these stellar and planetary Gods who had the making of all the transient, mortal creatures on earth.

The world, then, is basically a number of radiant energy sources, like suns, but these powers are not in time and are not apprehensible through the senses. The nearest approach to them in the sensible world are the stars and planets in their courses. Everything else in creations was patterned after one or several of these divine energies. Every mineral, jewel, plant, insect, animal and human being represented one or more of the divine natures.

This is a very different way of thinking about causation. The moving of a billiard ball is an event and that may cause other events, and we may trace them all back to the big bang. In the Homeric vision the created universe is the immediate expression in time of energies which are themselves in eternity. We see Hephaestus at work on the pentagonal dodecahedron of the outermost universe and powering the fixed stars to run in and out of the planets and back again. Plotinus supposed that Eternal Ideas contemplate themselves, and their rapture is so deep that the created world is its spontaneous precipitate. The created world in all its beauty and organization springs from that contemplation without effort or forethought.

Like everything else in time humans are images or versions of the Gods. This is not a presumptuous claim because every other creature is also an image or version of a God, or Gods. Like many of those creatures we are born to act and these actions image the various forms of the divine action which is no action because it is not in time. The kinds of human work are typified by the Olympians who eternally create, practise or sponsor them. The Olympians work because they are those operations and for no other purpose. Similarly the human worker ideally works only to work and we all know this disinterested worker in ourselves. That is when delight in the work completely absorbs us and we do, indeed, lose all sense of time.

Socrates thought himself an agent of Apollo, appointed by the Delphic Oracle. He was exceptionally assiduous in his duties. He inured himself to going without sleep or nourishment, never succumbed to drunkenness, swore that bare feet were the best means of coping with the snow, and kept himself primed and ready at all times for a streetside debate. He told his jurors at his trial that there was no point in their offering to let him go free on condition that he ceased his questioning of other people. He had been appointed to this task by Apollo, he believed, and, like any soldier on the battlefield, he could not depart from his place until ordered to do so by the God who put him there. Faithful unto death, he never received a penny for his teaching.

Socrates did not look much like Apollo. His eyes protruded so far, people said he could see round corners. Alcibiades thought Socrates godlike but insisted that Socrates confess that he looked like a woodland satyr. Alcibiades added that Socrates was one of those satyrs made out of clay which could be bought in the marketplace. These clay figures opened and inside each was a small but beautiful statue of a God or Goddess. Socrates, according to Alcibiades, was a rough diamond. Socrates was a sculptor's son who gave up a respectable living to take to the streets. There survives a stone statue of two Graces, attributed to Socrates. But he thought sculpting less Apollonian than publicly and privately questioning others.

He doubted sometimes that he had done his duty by Apollo. In his last months he turned to versifying Aesop's fables just in case he had not met the demands of a dream. He had had the dream all his life and it had told him 'Practise the Arts'. He had thought mostly that his life of questioning was being encouraged by the dream. But in his last days he was not so sure, and so he turned to versifying.

How Apollonian was Socrates' vocation? It is not easy to see how that long round of questioning in and out of so many houses, the palaestra, the streets, the law courts, how that realizes Apollo or any other of the Olympians. There was the tenuous link to Delphi's maxim 'Know thyself' and the fact that the Oracle had made clear that there was no one wiser than Socrates. But it was a huge step from that to the life that Socrates chose to lead. Socrates' vocation was highly unusual. It was also very hard to understand as a mission on behalf of Apollo. It seems that Socrates had even less reason than most of us to believe that he had found his God-given course of life.

There was his little voice which never told him what to do, only what not to do. So perhaps he forever found himself uncomfortable at whatever he worked, but he found his questioning of others was not interdicted by the voice. Socrates taught for no pay the art of knowing that you know nothing. Still, he had some vigorous successors and not only Plato. On the streets Diogenes outdid Socrates by living in a barrel in the Agora. Socrates had a home and Xanthippe and the children. But Diogenes took his school's name from Socrates' favorite oath 'By the Dog' and called himself a Cynic. In his ironic misrepresentations of popular opinion, Diogenes was very like Socrates, a Dionysian figure to Plato's Apollo. And we are back to those satyr statues which hold a fairer God within.

As Pythagoras was the founder of mathematics and Moses of Jewish law, so Socrates was the founder of ethics, according to tradition. He is the one through whom God handed down a great teaching to humankind. Pythagoras, it is said, studied with the Delphic priestess, Themistocleia. Socrates' connection with Delphi was through a friend who had reported only the Oracle's 'There is no one wiser than Socrates'. But this, with the little voice, was enough to set him on his course. In the brilliant Athens of the later fifth century, Socrates worked to demonstrate the universal ignorance of his neighbors as he had demonstrated his own ignorance to himself. For how many years had Socrates examined himself, and how strenuously, to acquire those dialectical powers? Here at last is the specific connection to Apollo among the Olympians. Socrates brought to moral debate the same rigor which Pythagoras had brought to plane geometry. Socrates founded a new science, as Apollonian as astronomy, geometry or music, because ethics, too, was a model of intellectual precision. Strange now to think of ethics as an exact science.

The cool logic of the theorem is the form of ethics as Socrates taught it. In geometry the content of the science is lines, angles, shapes. In Socratic ethics, the content is the theory of work. How and why we work is almost the whole of Socratic ethics. Does this mean that he did know something despite his denials? He understood the logical relations between the terms of the Greek moral vocabulary. He was also expert in the language and theory of knowledge. His terminological rigor enabled him to refute any claims to knowledge by his interlocutors. He was an excellent detector of incoherences in other people's opinions. He was famous for how his simple talk of carpenters and doctors completely undermined the sophisticated and grandiloquent, and had a compelling attraction all its own.

Why is Apollo god of geometry, astronomy, music and ethics? On the temple of Zeus at Olympia Apollo is standing at the apex of a pediment, one hand thrust out against a rearing centaur's face. Apollo is utterly calm, the centaur orgiastic. Apollo is measure, stillness at the center. There clarity returns and the most perfect precision, either in the exact measurement of intervals or in the logic of a vocabulary's entailment. The Sun's movements were the supreme instance of this precision, and they in turn were exemplified by Odysseus' shooting of the arrow through the twelve axeheads on the feast day of Apollo. I like to think of that Apollo at Olympia as the very moment of the winter solstice when the retreat of the sun is halted and it begins its half year's return. The centaur is incipient chaos but the exactness of the Sun's schedule does not so much halt as transcend it.

I have dwelt on Plato's vision of Socrates because Plato is the most comprehensive philosopher of work in our era and Socrates is his paragon. In Socrates Plato has drawn an inward portrait of how a vocation is born, develops and defines itself. To see Socrates at work is to see why Plato thought that the realization of our vocations was the primary task of a civilized society, however unusual Socrates' own vocation was. Plato divided his ideal city state into classes because he supposed every human collective produces talents as they are needed. The fulfillment of these various capacities for work was the unique requirement for a happy society. But these talents are also divine and so are we. In the *Phaedrus* Socrates describes a sequence of eleven Gods and Goddesses, each of whom at their time rises to the summit of the heavens and breaks into the beyond.[1] In the trains and retinues of these eleven, humankind follows and each of us in our turn may rise with our God or Goddess to that summit and see beyond.

Socrates accounted himself in the retinue of Apollo, as had Pythagoras and Parmenides. In the Greek Anthology there are poems by shepherds dedicating their crooks, pipes and scrips to Pan on their retiring after a life's work. What happens when a musician performs well in public? Inspiration? Has the God been breathed in? Or is this rather a glimpse at the core of a God who is always there. Plotinus says that the art is always more fully in the artist or practitioner than ever it is in any work. Plato describes a stone of Magnesia which attracts iron rings to itself and they hang from it as if attached. And the force from the stone passes through those rings so that they may hold other iron rings to themselves as they are held to the stone. This is an image of Homer's relation to the Muse and of ours to Homer.

Work is an opportunity for enthusiasm. It is purely a service, to the presiding divinity on the one hand and to the client on the other. No craft or profession is in the least concerned with the advantage or interest of its practitioner, but only with those of its customer. The earning of wages is therefore incidental to the crafts and professions, another skill altogether according to Plato. And when we see the mad disparities between services and wages, Plato

1. Plato, *Phaedrus*, 25.

has a point. But selfless expertise is its own reward. Aristotle explains pleasure as 'unhindered activity' which may describe the bliss of the devoted and expert worker. To the novice the disciplines of a craft or profession are as uncomfortable and unyielding as the leather of army boots. But once the boots have broken in their wearer, that very harshness in the leather becomes its strength. Our individual capacities to bend to the rigors of one or other of the crafts and professions mark the tiny deity within the clay of each of us. The unending stream of the generations always provides its doctors, scholars, lawyers, musicians, whose practices have been venerated from ancient times and bound close with oaths. To marry such work is to die as an individual and to be reborn as a professional, and these initiation rites are still performed in graduation ceremonies universally. A short journey across the stage is the end of one life and the beginning of another.

And so we answer the challenge to Socrates made by Adeimantus and Glaucon: why be ethical even unto a terrible death? When the senior law officers of a tyrannized country suffer ignominy, torture and death rather than walk away or deliver evil law; when a nurse works to help the victims of a plague against which there is no protection; when a priest or preacher endures prison and execution rather than abuse or forsake the faith; when soldiers die for their country from agonizing wounds: all this is nothing extraordinary. It is what they have been striving to achieve all their working lives. Properly to follow a profession is precisely this making over of the egoic self and the physical life to the ideals of the work, the gaining of selflessness through dedication. What, then if the occasion demands the actual sacrifice? In some professions, exactly how this ultimate sacrifice is realized in eternity has been made very clear. The martyred teacher joins the communion of saints; the fallen Greek warrior is worshipped like a God in the rituals of the hero. It is not the dying which we need fear, however horrible. What we must fear is that we fail the ideal of our profession in that crisis, and choose what we are not at the price of who we are.

In the west the ethical masters of our two major traditions, Socrates and Jesus, both paid the final price in the performance of their missions. The Greco-Roman and the Judaeo-Christian legacies are identical in this. Jesus' fate is even closer to the tormented just man of Adeimantus and Glaucon than the fate of Socrates himself.

12

PLATO'S NUMBER OF JUSTICE

Plato's account of Justice in the *Republic*, though long, seems more limited than some fragments of his predecessors. Compare for example fragment 94 of Heraclitus:

> *The sun will not transgress his measures: otherwise the Furies, ministers of Justice, will find him out;*[1]

and lines thirteen to fifteen of fragment 8 of Parmenides:

> *So far as that is concerned Justice has never released Being in its fetters either to come into being or to perish, but holds it fast;*[2]

and Aristotle's statement that the Pythagoreans believed Justice a number equal times equal.[3]

Plato's predecessors held theories in which Justice plays a cosmic role, organizes or maintains an equilibrium at the heart of things. The *Republic*, on the other hand, seems a discussion of Justice as the principle of organization only in the human state or soul; Plato does not there appear to ascribe to Justice a role in the more general dispositions of the intelligible and visible worlds.

This limitation on Plato's discussion of Justice in the *Republic* is strange. The Republic is not confined in its themes to those of human soul and state; books 6 and 7, for example, are a most thorough account in ontology and epistemology, the Sun and the Good, the Divided Line, and the Cave. There is enough room here for Justice to play a larger part. The omission of any important role for

1. K. Freeman, tr. *Ancilla to the Presocratic Philosophers*, 1948, Oxford, p. 31.
2. Ibid., p. 43.
3. Aristotle, *Magna Moralia*, 1, 1182A.14.

Justice in these passages is still more strange since here Plato, like his predecessors, propounds a belief in a rational world-order imposed by and accessible to a divine intelligence. With these views the notion that Justice has a part in cosmic as well as human organization is not just consistent but almost identical.

It could be that Plato in the *Republic* is not more limiting than his predecessors, but like them ascribes a cosmological role to Justice. How he may do it is the subject of this essay. The argument of the essay is partly deductive and of mathematical certainty and clarity, but it contains no proof that Plato intended the consequences of his theories here deduced. Perhaps he did intend them but if he did, he chose not to declare it. Still, even if Plato did not intend these consequences, I hope the account I give of them here would please him. Since the intention cannot be proven, this account must follow the method of hypothesis: show where his argument leads, presume he intended it to do so, and then show what would follow from such a presumption. If the hypothesis generates consequences which do not conflict with Plato's expressed views but support and promote them, then that is some reason for adopting it. If it provides solutions to problems not solved in any other way, then that may be a better reason. Perhaps also a reason can be found for Plato's failure to declare these consequences of his argument himself.

Socrates is pressed by Glaucon to say more of Sun and Good.[4] Socrates tells him to take a line, divide it, then divide each of the two sections in the same proportion. This procedure generates a line of four parts, and these four parts are related to each other in the same way as the four kinds of human understanding are related to each other and to the Good. There is a consequence of this procedure, as follows: if the parts of the Line are given whole number values according to these proportions; if these four numbers have no factor in common, and are in their simplest expression: then the sum of these four numbers is the square number of a whole number. The same number of pebbles used to illustrate the Line may be reformed into a square. This consequence follows whether the divisions of the Line are equal or unequal, but is interesting only where they are unequal.

4. Plato, *Republic*, 509c, 5–8.

First a demonstration that this is a consequence of so dividing the Line, and that Plato could have known it to be so. That the consequence holds in particular cases is easily seen. For example, let the Line be divided in the proportions 6:3 and the two sections so formed be divided in the proportions 4:2 and 2:1. Then 4+2+2+1 equal 9, the square of the whole number 3. Here is an algebraic proof:

> Let there be four whole numbers a, b, c, and d, such that $a/b = c/d = a+b/c+d$ and a, b, c, and d have no factor in common. Then $ad = bc$; $a(c+d) = b(a+b)$. So $ac+bc = b(a+b)$. So, since $a+b$ is not 0, $c = b$. So the hypotheses reduce to $ad = b^2$; a, b, and d have no common factor. Then if p divides a and d, p^2 divides b^2, so p divides b. So a and d have no common factor. Now b divides ad, so write $b = b_1$, b_2 where b_1 and b_2 are whole numbers and $b1$ divides a, b_2 divides d. Then $ad = b_1^2$, b_2^2. So $a+b+c+d = b_1^2+2b_1$, $b_2+b_2^2 = (b_1+b_2)^2$. But since b_1, b_2 are whole numbers, b_1+b_2 is a whole number. So the sum of the four numbers a, b, c, and d is the square number of a whole number.[5]

This proof is not stated in terms Plato used. But in another form it is like many by Euclid for example. Compare *Elements* 2:4, 8:11, 10:117. Russell and Heath give algebraic paraphrases of these proofs of Euclid which bear a resemblance to the one given above.[6] Heath remarks that the Greeks possessed

> ...a geometrical algebra which indeed by Euclid's time (and probably long before) had reached such a stage of development that it could solve the same problems as our algebra so far as they do not involve the manipulation of expressions of a degree higher than the second.[7]

5. By J. Groves, Dept. of Mathematics, Melbourne University. For b = c see also J. Adam, *The Republic of Plato*, 1921, Cambridge, ii.64.

6. See e.g., B. Russell, *History of Western Philosophy*, 1961, London, p. 54 and footnote: T. Heath, *Euclid's Elements*, 1956, New York, i. 374–381, ii. 363f: T. Heath, *Greek Mathematics*, 1960, Oxford, i.91.

7. T. Heath, *Euclid's Elements*, i. 372.

So the theorem and its proof are not obviously beyond Plato's power. Plato himself could have devised the theorem since other theorems about square numbers are traditionally attributed to him. For example, at *Timaeus* 32 Timaeus tells Socrates that between two plane numbers there is only one mean number. Heath takes Plato's plane numbers to mean square numbers and notes that Nicomachus attributed theorem 8:11 in Euclid's *Elements* to Plato. Proclus attributes to Plato a method for discovering sets of three whole numbers which can be the sides of a right-angled triangle. According to Heath, this method was probably derived from a consideration of square numbers and their gnomons represented by dots or pebbles.[8] Equally, contemplation of these figures could generate the theorem proved algebraically above.

The divisions of the Line Plato expresses as a series of ratios in the manner of Euclid. These ratios are intended to represent a series of imitations. How? If sets of things replace the magnitudes of the Line, perhaps the smallest set is multiplied the same number of times to produce the second smallest as is the third to produce the fourth and the first and second to produce the third and fourth. If there are x dianoetic images to every one form, then there are x visible images to every one visible object, and x^2 visible images to every one form. This is unlikely to be what Plato meant.

Keats has an image:

> *And haply the Queen-Moon is on her throne*
> *Cluster'd around by all her starry Fays.*[9]

As moon to stars, so queen to fairies. But Keats does not mean strictly to compare the quantities. Moon and stars, queen and fairies are not compared because there is one moon, one queen and as many stars as fairies, but because queen and fairies are disposed in relation to each other as moon to stars, in a kind of spatial fealty. As the two dispositions are felt to be similar, so the image is felt to be exact. Such images succeed whatever the relations or ratios between the items of each group, provided only these relations or ratios are

8. *Euclid's Elements*, op. cit., ii. 294; *Greek Mathematics*, i. 89.
9. J. Keats, *Ode to a Nightingale*, 36–37.

parallel. The ratios of the Line do not represent similar numbers or dispositions in space but similar kinds of imitating and imitation, and there are more of them than in Keats' image. There moon and stars are related to each other merely as fairy-queen to fairies, but in Plato's image the intelligible and visible worlds are themselves related to each other as their members among themselves. And so we see how the visible world is so perfect a representation of the intelligible world that it even contains within itself reflections as an image of its own relation to that intelligible world.

My hypothesis is that Plato intended the divisions of the Line to have the mathematical consequences deduced above. The account of the Line is then comparable to his predecessors' accounts of Justice. For the Pythagoreans Justice is a number equal times equal. The Line is such a number, so Justice is the number of the Line. Justice is as much the coordinating principle of the parts of the Line as of the parts of human state and soul. The quadripartite division of the state into four classes and the tripartite division of the soul are complemented by this further division of the modes of cognition into four distinct but related categories. For Parmenides Justice holds Being fast in mighty bonds. In the *Timaeus* the best bond is said to be the accomplishment of proportion.[10] For Parmenides the binding power is Justice: perhaps too Justice is Plato's binding of being and becoming in his dialogue on Justice. Plato's dividing of the Line imposes determinate limits on a previously undifferentiated continuum, marking measures beyond which the measured may not go. This is comparable to Heraclitus' theory that Justice prevents the sun from overstepping its measures.

Where is Justice on the Line? The intelligible sections seem exclusively mathematical. This omission of Justice is odd in a dialogue on Justice, here explaining the knowledge which the ruler must have to rule justly. Plato often claims that to be virtuous one must know virtue. But on the hypothesis Justice is accounted for: not itself located on any part of the Line, it is the structure of the Line and of the universe which the Line illustrates. This Justice the philosopher contemplates, and this contemplation unfits him temporarily for

10. Plato, *Timaeus*, 31C, 1–4.

legal disputation about the statues and shadows of Justice in the Cave. Perhaps for Plato anyone who does not see the consequences of his so dividing the Line does not see Justice itself. Obvious from one point of view but not from the Cave, Plato does not choose to explain it.

Plato's Line may be represented as a square of dots or pebbles, e.g.

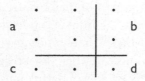

where a = 4, b = 2, c = 2, d = 1, the divisions corresponding to the divisions of the Line. The four orders of the intelligible and visible worlds are represented by the four parts of the square in mutual proportion. Let the square a in the diagram stand for the forms; b, c and d for the other three orders of being. Then b, c, and d together make a gnomon to the square a. A scholiast to Euclid writes that the name of the gnomon

> came from its incidental property, namely that from it the whole is known, whether of the whole area, or of the remainder when it is either placed round or taken away.[11]

The point of the remark is that the word 'gnomon' appears to derive from a common Greek verb meaning 'to know', and to be formed by the addition of an ending which denotes an active agent—hence 'knower'. If Plato intended his divisions of the Line to make a gnomon and a square and if he took the derivation of the word 'gnomon' seriously, then he may be illustrating how the three sets of things, b, c, and d, are a means by which the forms, a, are known. Or again how the forms, together with the material world they generate, reconstitute the overall shape of the forms by themselves.

11. *Scholium* 2, no. 11, Euclid, Editor: Heiberg, v. 225; Heath, *Euclid's Elements*, i. 371.

Socrates uses the division of the Line to illustrate a difficult distinction between philosophical and mathematical knowledge. From the postulates of mathematics, the line, the square and so on, the philosopher 'ascends' where the mathematician 'descends.' Could it be that realizing how the divisions of the Line makes a square is an instance of philosophical 'ascension'? Clearly it is not the simple apprehension of the theorem that such divisions constitute a square which matters here. That is part of mathematics. But the apprehension that the four modes of human understanding are bound together so closely, and their corresponding objects likewise, this apprehension begins to meet that hardest criticism of Plato's cosmology: why, if the forms are so wonderful, have a created world at all? Now the orders of being and becoming are spread out in their relations before us and we see that nothing is lost to us in overall perfection by this addition of the creation, and a new intellectual beauty is gained. It is hard usually to accept Plato's distinctions between the more and the less real, but in this passage the 'levels' of reality are so united that we accept their gradations for the pleasure of seeing their harmony.

13

PLATO'S SONG
OF THE SIRENS

The Song of the Sirens

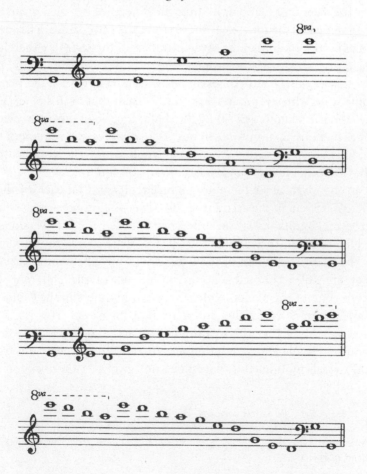

This composition is derived from Plato's comments on the eight Sirens in the Myth of Er and his account of the seven Circles of the Different in the *Timaeus*.[1] As Timaeus explains it, the circuits of the planets correspond to the series 1, 2, 3, 4, 9, 8, 27. In this composition, the ratio 1:2 realizes the octave, so that the first two numbers of the series are realized by the same tone played in consecutive octaves. Here the higher note, the shorter string, is the smaller number and the lower note, the longer, string is the larger number.[2] 3 is the arithmetic mean between 2 and 4, so is expressed by the fifth of the second octave as 4 is represented by a return to the tone of 2 and 1, now in the third octave. 8 is the same tone in the fourth octave and 9 is the second of that octave since the difference between 9 and 8 is the interval of the tone. 27 is the sixth in the fifth octave. The seven tones corresponding to the seven numbers of the series are therefore the octave (1, 2, 4, 8), the fifth (3), the second (9) and the sixth (27). On this account Plato's tones all fall within what we call the pentatonic scale, which is paradoxical to the extent that in this passage of the *Timaeus* Plato is describing the diatonic scale of the octave. In so far as there are no semitones in our series of notes, each circuit of the Different is represented by a pure whole tone. The composition above follows this rule and makes no use of semitones.

In the Myth of Er there are eight circuits and on each of them there is a Siren. In the account of the *Timaeus*, numbers are ascribed to seven circuits only. The difference between the two versions is explained by the inclusion in the Myth of Er of a Siren for the Circle of the Same, the circuit of the fixed stars. Since these are invariant, they are not accounted among the circuits of the Different, the seven rings of the planets which are given numbers in the *Timaeus*. The fixed stars have a ring and a Siren of their own. This ring, the largest, holds all the others within it and carries them round with its motion. The planetary variations are merely minor departures from this overall motion. But Plato does not give us a number for the

---

1. Plato, *Republic*, 617; *Timaeus*, 35–36.
2. According to Theon of Smyrna, Plato ascribes the largest numbers to the lowest note: *Mathematics Useful for the Study of Plato*, tr. R. & D. Lawlor, 1980, San Diego, p. 43.

Siren who sings on the Circle of the Same. My own suggestion is 64, the repetition of the tone of 1, 2, 4, and 8 in the seventh octave. Where 2 and 3 are linear numbers, 4 and 9 plane or square numbers, and 8 and 27 solid or cube numbers, 64 is the first number which is both plane and solid, square and cube. To realize the identity of the astronomical and musical conformations, the composition should be played on an organ and the tone in the seventh octave should be sustained throughout. If played on a piano, this note should be sustained and replayed as often as necessary to sound continuously.[3]

3. I am grateful to Mr. John O'Donnell for his scoring of the composition.

Made in United States
North Haven, CT
28 October 2022